In a Prominent Bar in Secau

Johns Hopkins: Poetry and Fiction

John T. Irwin, General Editor

Books by X. J. Kennedy

VERSE
Nude Descending a Staircase
Growing into Love
Breaking and Entering
Three Tenors, One Vehicle (with
    James Camp and Keith Waldrop)
Emily Dickinson in Southern
    California
Cross Ties
Dark Horses
The Lords of Misrule
Peeping Tom's Cabin
In a Prominent Bar in Secaucus

VERSE FOR CHILDREN
One Winter Night in August
The Phantom Ice Cream Man
Did Adam Name the Vinegarroon?
The Forgetful Wishing Well
The Beasts of Bethlehem
The Kite That Braved Old Orchard
    Beach
Ghastlies, Goops, and Pincushions
Uncle Switch
Brats
Fresh Brats
Drat These Brats
Elympics
Elefantina's Dream
Exploding Gravy

ANTHOLOGIES FOR CHILDREN
Knock at a Star (with Dorothy M.
    Kennedy)
Talking Like the Rain (with
    Dorothy M. Kennedy)

FICTION FOR CHILDREN
The Owlstone Crown
The Eagle as Wide as the World

VERSE ANTHOLOGIES
Tygers of Wrath
Pegasus Descending (with James
    Camp and Keith Waldrop)

TEXTBOOKS
Mark Twain's Frontier (with James
    Camp)
Messages
An Introduction to Poetry (with
    Dana Gioia)
An Introduction to Fiction (with
    Dana Gioia)
Literature (with Dana Gioia)
Handbook of Literary Terms (with
    Dana Gioia and Mark Bauerlein)
The Bedford Reader (with
    Dorothy M. Kennedy and
    Jane E. Aaron)
The Bedford Guide for College
    Writers (with Dorothy M.
    Kennedy, Marcia F. Muth, and
    Sylvia A. Holladay)
Writing and Revising (with
    Dorothy M. Kennedy and
    Marcia F. Muth)

TRANSLATION
Lysistrata, *by Aristophanes*

EDITIONS
Knee-Deep in Blazing Snow, *by*
    James Hayford (edited with
    Dorothy M. Kennedy)
Inside Man, *by George Fox*

In a Prominent Bar in Secaucus

New and Selected Poems, 1955–2007

X. J. Kennedy

The Johns Hopkins University Press
Baltimore

This book has been brought to publication with the generous assistance of the Albert Dowling Trust.

The Johns Hopkins University Press
2715 North Charles Street
Baltimore, Maryland 21218-4363
www.press.jhu.edu

Library of Congress Cataloging-in-Publication Data

Kennedy, X. J.
In a prominent bar in Secaucus : new and selected poems, 1955–2007 / X. J. Kennedy.
    p.   cm. — (Johns Hopkins, poetry and fiction)
Includes index.
ISBN-13: 978-0-8018-8653-9 (acid-free paper)
ISBN-10: 0-8018-8653-8 (acid-free paper)
ISBN-13: 978-0-8018-8654-6 (pbk. : acid-free paper)
ISBN-10: 0-8018-8654-6 (pbk. : acid-free paper)
I. Title.
PS3521.E56315 2007
811'.54—dc22   2006103114

For Dorothy, as ever

Contents

Slim Volumes

Breaking and Entering (1971)

Emily Dickinson in Southern California (1973)

The Lords of Misrule (2002)

New Poems

Nude Descending a Staircase (1961)

First Confession

Blood thudded in my ears. I scuffed,
    Steps stubborn, to the telltale booth
Beyond whose curtained portal coughed
    The robed repositor of truth.

The slat shot back. The universe
    Bowed down his cratered dome to hear
Enumerated my each curse,
    The sip snitched from my old man's beer,

My sloth pride envy lechery,
    The dime held back from Peter's Pence
With which I'd bribed my girl to pee
    That I might spy her instruments.

Hovering scale-pans when I'd done
    Settled their balance slow as silt
While in the restless dark I burned
    Bright as a brimstone in my guilt

Until as one feeds birds he doled
    Seven Our Fathers and one Hail
Which I to double-scrub my soul
    Intoned twice at the altar rail

Where Sunday in seraphic light
    I knelt, as full of grace as most,
And stuck my tongue out at the priest:
    A fresh roost for the Holy Ghost.

Solitary Confinement

She might have stolen from his arms
Except that there was nothing left
To steal. There was the crucifix
Of silver good enough to hock,
But how far could she go on it
And what had he left her to pack
And steal away with and lay down
By someone new in a new town?

She put the notion back
And turned her look up where the clock,
Green ghost, swept round its tethered hand
That had made off with many nights
But no more could break from its shelf
Than she could from this bed where breath
By breath these years he'd nailed her fast
Between two thieves, him and herself.

On a Child Who Lived One Minute

Into a world where children shriek like suns
Sundered from other suns on their arrival,
She stared, and saw the waiting shape of evil,
But couldn't take its meaning in at once,
So fresh her understanding, and so fragile.

Her first breath drew a fragrance from the air
And put it back. However hard her agile
Heart danced, however full the surgeon's satchel
Of healing stuff, a blackness tiptoed in her
And snuffed the only candle of her castle.

Oh, let us do away with elegiac
Drivel. Who can restore a thing so brittle,
So new in any jingle? Still, I marvel
That, making light of mountainloads of logic,
So much could stay a moment in so little.

Faces from a Bestiary

suggested by the twelfth-century
Livre des Créatures *of Philip de Thaun*

1
The Lion sleeps with open eyes
That none may take him by surprise.
The Son of God he signifies,

For when a Lion stillborn lies
His mother circles him and cries.
Then on the third day he will rise.

2
Hyena is a beast to hate.
No man hath seen him copulate.
He is unto himself a mate.

You who this creature emulate,
Who with your mirrors fornicate,
Do not repent. It is too late.

Nude Descending a Staircase

Toe upon toe, a snowing flesh,
A gold of lemon, root and rind,
She sifts in sunlight down the stairs
With nothing on. Nor on her mind.

We spy beneath the banister
A constant thresh of thigh on thigh—
Her lips imprint the swinging air
That parts to let her parts go by.

One-woman waterfall, she wears
Her slow descent like a long cape
And pausing, on the final stair
Collects her motions into shape.

The Autumn in Norfolk Shipyard

is a secret one infers
from camouflage. Scrap steel
betrays no color of season,
corrosion works year-round.
But in sandblasted stubble
lurks change: parched thistle-burr,
blown milkweed hull—dried potholes
after tides reassume their foam.

Destroyers mast to mast,
mechanical conifers,
bear pointed lights. Moored tankers
redden slow as leaves.
Under the power crane
dropped girders lie like twigs.
In drydock ripened tugs
burst pod-wide—ringbolts bobble
to quiet upon steel-plate
mud. A flake of paint falls,
green seas spill last year's needles.

Warning to Sculptors

Croon to the stone that draws
Your dull hand onward. Supplicate
Galatea till of her own choice
She let fall from her lines
Stone swaddles with bumbling clatter,
Into your arms glide forth,
Only a cloth of marble dust
Across concessive loins.

But let you once run hand
Across pores breathing in her cheek
And smile and say, I made me this—
Then shall you rut in stone,
Shall stone give birth to stone,
Stone swing cradled in stone arms,
To cold bald stone stone croon
And stone to ravenous stone give suck.

Lewis Carroll

Click! down the black whiterabbithole
Of his lighttight box he scooped
Liddell girls (women in capsule form,
My dears, the better to eat you).

On tiptoe past intimidated primroses,
His head ateeter on its collar wall,
The Reverend Mister Dodgson longdivided
God's cipher (1 goes 3 × into 3)

And shrinking as his Alice grew, rejected
The little flask of love that said *Drink Me*.

II

In a Prominent Bar in Secaucus One Day

To the tune of "The Old Orange Flute"
or "Sweet Betsy from Pike"

In a prominent bar in Secaucus one day
Rose a lady in skunk with a topheavy sway,
Raised a knobby red finger—all turned from their beer—
While with eyes bright as snowcrust she sang high and clear:

"Now who of you'd think from an eyeload of me
That I once was a lady as proud as can be?
Oh, I'd never sit down by a tumbledown drunk
If it wasn't, my dears, for the high price of junk.

"All the gents used to swear that the white of my calf
Beat the down of the swan by a length and a half.
In the kerchief of linen I caught to my nose
Ah, there never fell snot, but a little gold rose.

"I had seven gold teeth and a toothpick of gold,
My Virginia cheroot was a leaf of it rolled
And I'd light it each time with a thousand in cash—
Why, the bums used to fight if I flicked them an ash.

"Once the toast of the Biltmore, the belle of the Taft,
I would drink bottle beer at the Drake, never draft,
And dine at the Astor on Salisbury steak
With a clean tablecloth for each bite I did take.

"In a car like the Roxy I'd roll to the track
With a steel-guitar trio, a bar in the back,
And the wheels made no noise, they turned over so fast,
Still it took you ten minutes to see me go past.

"When the horses bowed down to me that I might choose,
I'd bet on them all, for I hated to lose.
Now I'm saddled each night for my butter and eggs
And the broken threads race down the backs of my legs.

"Let you hold in mind, girls, that your beauty must pass
Like a lovely white clover that rusts with its grass.
Keep your bottoms off bar stools and marry you young
Or be left an old barrel with many a bung.

"For when time takes you out for a spin in his car
You'll be hard-pressed to stop him from going too far
And be left by the roadside, for all your good deeds,
Two toadstools for tits and a face full of weeds."

All the house raised a cheer, but the man at the bar
Made a phonecall and up pulled a red patrol car
And she blew us a kiss as they copped her away
From that prominent bar in Secaucus, N.J.

Barking Dog Blues

I hear those barking dog blues
Every getting-out-of-bed of day,
Hear those barking dog blues
Every getting-out-of-bed of day,
Barking dog blues
That chase my other blues away.

Mister Municipal Dog Catcher,
Won't you throw me in your pound?
'Cause I just might bite somebody
If you leave me running round.

Baby, some men want to marry—
Me, I'd rather go to jail.
You drive me round in circles
Like a tin can tied to my tail.

Quit your messing round my little dog
'Cause my big dog's got a bone.
If you don't want my big dog
Leave my little dog alone.

Hear me barking Monday morning
In the driving rain.
I'll lay down in your kennel
But I won't wear your chain.

Inscriptions after Fact

for Frank Brownlow

1
Lilith

Adam's first wife had soft lips but no soul.
He looked her in the eye, back looked a hole.
Her small ear lay, a dry well so profound
No word he pebbled in it made a sound.

Could he complete what God had left half-wrought?
He practiced in a looking lake, he taught
Her rudiments of wriggle, how to stand
On liltless feet. She handed him her hand.

Her breasts stood up, but in them seemed to rise
No need for man. He roamed lone in her thighs
And inmost touching, most knew solitude.
In vacant rooms, on whom can one intrude?

*O let down mercy on a man who clings
To echoes, beds him with imaginings!
Sweet Lord,* he prayed, *with what shade do I lie?*
Second came she whom he begot us by.

2
The Sirens

stayed in one place and did no work
But warble ditties a bit loose,
Strike poses, primp, bedeck their rock
With primrose boxes. Odysseus

Salt-lipped, long bandied before winds,
Heard in his loins a bass chord stir,

Said to his men, "Men, stop your ears—
I need not, being an officer."

Under the deaf indifferent tread
Of wood on water, round each oar
Broke like the grapes of Ilium
Ripening clusters of blue air

And when those soft sounds stole, there grew
The notion as he champed his bit
That love was all there was, and death
Had something to be said for it.

Roared as the music sweetened, railed
Against his oarsmen's bent wet slopes,
Imprisoned in propriety
And pagan ethic. Also ropes.

Sails strummed. The keel drove tapestries
Of distance on the sea's silk-loom
Leaving those simple girls beyond
Woven undone rewoven foam

To wonder: had they lost their touch?
Unbroken yet, a woof of sea
Impelled him to his dying dog,
Pantoufles, and Penelope.

3
Narcissus Suitor

He touched her face and gooseflesh crept—
He loved her, as it were,
Not for her look though it lay deep
But what he saw in her.

Drew her up wobbling in his arms,
Laid lips by her smooth cheek,
And would have joined the two of him
In one cohesive Greek

When soft by his obdurate ear
Like lips two ripples pursed,
And syllables distinct and pure
Bubbled to air and burst:

"Oh, keep your big feet to yourself,
Good sir, goddammit, stop!
I'm not that sort of pool at all!
I'll scream! I'll call a cop!

"Settle me back in my right bed
Or you shall edge your skiff
Through ice possessive as your eyes,
As blue, as frozen stiff."

4
Theater of Dionysus

Athens, U.S. Sixth Fleet

On a stone bench by an aisle
In the Theater of Dionysus
I make a flock of Greek kids smile
Sketching them Mickey Mouses

Where beery Aristophanes
By sanction till night's fall
Ribbed Eleusinian mysteries
With queer-joke and pratfall.

From the sacked Parthenon on high
A bird serenely warbles.
Sellers of paperweights resell
The Elgin marbles.

Here where queen-betrayed
Agamemnon had to don
Wine-purple robes, boys in torn drabs
Try my whitchat on,

Over stones where Orestes fled
The gibber of the Furies
Girls hawking flyspecked postcards
Pursue the tourist.

Here in painted anguish-mask
Andromache
Mourned her slain son—"Young man,
Aren't you from Schenectady?"

As I trudge down, a pebble breaks
Rattling across stone tiers,
Scattering echoes. Did I kick
Some watcher's skull downstairs?

Silence imponders back.
I take the stage, the pebble
Stilled on a lower tier.
Trailing home now, the child rabble.

I stand in the center of the stage,
Could speak, but the sun's setting
In back of neon signs. Night unsheathes
Her chill blade. Better be getting

Back to my radared bark—
No thresh of oars, sails with gods' crests.
Does the wind stir through the dark
Or does a throng of ghosts?

I run. Inaudible laughter drives
Offstage my spirit
As in the parched grass, wind routs
A white shiver before it.

At the Stoplight by the Paupers' Graves

Earth has been saved them but they won't give in,
Won't lie down quiet as they did before,
Though all is as it was: two scrawny kids
To a bed and the rat-wind scudding at the door.

Skull against skull, they won't stretch out at ease
Their jammed arms, won't set grass to root for good.
Perennials that came up only once
Struggle and dry down from their stones of wood.

My engine shudders as if about to stall,
But I've no heart to wait with them all night.
That would be long to tense here for a leap,
Thrall to the remote decisions of the light.

Little Elegy

for a child who skipped rope

Here lies resting, out of breath
Out of turns, Elizabeth
Whose quicksilver toes not quite
Cleared the whirring edge of night.

Earth whose circles round us skim
Till they catch the lightest limb,
Shelter now Elizabeth
And for her sake trip up Death.

Ladies Looking for Lice

after Arthur Rimbaud, "Les Chercheuses de poux"

When the child's forehead is afire with red
Tortures and he longs for vague white dreams to come,
Two enchantress big sisters steal close to his bed
With tinselly fingers, nails of platinum.

By a casement thrown open they sit the child down
Where blue air bathes stealthily the budded stalk
And in his locks thick with dew and along his crown
Their sorceress hands thin and terrible walk.

He traces the song of their hesitant breath,
Spumed honey that sends forth slow tendrils, the hiss
That now and then breaks it: spit blown through the teeth
And sucked back on the lips, or desire for a kiss.

He hears their black lashes beat through the perfume
Of the quiet and a crackle like static: the slice
Of their fingernails, queens of his indolent gloom,
Passing death sentences on little lice.

Now in him a wine mounts: laziness,
Sound that can drive mad, a harmonica sigh,
And the child feels in time to each slow caress
Rush and recede endlessly the desire to cry.

B Negative

M/60/5FT4/W/PROT

You know it's April by the falling-off
In coughdrop boxes—fewer people cough—
    By daisies' first white eyeballs in the grass
And every dawn more underthings cast off.

Now plum trees stretch recovered boughs to us
And doubledecked in green, the downtown bus.
    In this fresh season—so your stab-pole tells—
Love beds down, buds, and is deciduous.

I set down burlap bag. In pigeon talk
The wobbling pigeon flutes on the sidewalk,
    Struts in the breeze and clicks leisurely wings
As though the corn he ate grew on a stalk.

So plump he topples where he tries to stand,
He pecks my shoelaces, come to demand
    Another sack, another fifteen cents.
Oh well. Who else will eat out of my hand?

It used to be that when I laid my head
And body with it down by you in bed
    You did not turn from me nor fall to sleep
But turn to fall between my arms instead.

And now I lay bifocals down. My feet
Forget the route that brought me to your street.
    I can't make out your face for steamed-up glass
Nor quite call back your outline on the sheet.

I know how, bent to a movie magazine,
The hobo's head lights up, and from its screen

Imagined bosoms in slow motion bloom
And no director interrupts the scene.

I used to purchase in the Automat
A cup of soup and fan it with my hat
    Until a stern voice from the change booth crashed
Like nickels: *Gentlemen do not do that.*

Spring has no household, no abiding heat,
Pokes forth no bud from branches of concrete,
    Nothing to touch you, nothing you can touch.
The snow at least keeps track of people's feet.

The springer spaniel and the buoyant hare
Seem half at home reclining in mid-air,
    But Lord, the times I've leaped the way they do
And looked round for a foothold—in despair.

The all-night subway cheaper than a room,
I browse the *News*—or so the guards assume—
    And there, half waking, tucked in funny sheets,
Hurtle within a mile-a-minute womb.

Down streets that wake up earlier than wheels
The routed spirit flees on dusty heels
    And in the soft fire of a muscatel
Sits up, stretches forth fingertips, and feels—

Down streets so deep the sun can't vault their walls,
Where one-night wives make periodic calls,
    Where cat steals stone, where rat makes off with child,
And lyre and lute lie down under three balls,

Down blocks in sequence, fact by separate fact,
The human integers add and subtract

Till locked away in some flea-bag hotel
You wake one day to find yourself abstract

And turn a knob and hear a voice: *Insist*
On Jiffy Blades, they're tender to the wrist—
    Then static, then a squawk as if your hand
Had shut some human windpipe with a twist.

I know how, lurking under trees by dark,
Poor loony stranglers out to make their mark
    Reach forth shy hands to stroke some woman's hair—
I pick up after them in Central Park.

At the Ghostwriter's Deathbed

How many statesmen let you move their lips
    Like creaking shutters while they stood there dazed?
What statues did you dedicate? What ships
    Were launched with wind your cobbled speeches raised?

Off with you. Give our ears a bit of ease,
    Pack up your gibber, take it with you. You've
Graven your tombstone in officialese.
    Get under it. Go moan at one remove.

Incomplete spirit in a house laid waste,
    With thinning hands you tweeze threads in your sheet.
Little enough is left of you. The priest
    Forgives you, gives you flesh and blood to eat.

At cockcrow, helpless for a turn of phrase,
    A hollow teletype forgets to click.
Stiff is the air you tortured with clichés
    And tongueless stands the body politic.

You sigh between our lines. We can't erase
    Your one historic catchphrase. Worn to death,
It walks, a murmur from some public face.
    What made us think we'd boarded up your breath?

Rondel

Violation on a theme by Charles d'Orléans

The world is taking off her clothes
Of snowdrift, rain, and strait-laced freeze
And turns, to show forth by degrees
The bosom of a Rose La Rose.

There's not a bud nor bird, Lord knows,
Can keep still in its balconies.
The world is taking off her clothes
Of snowdrift, rain, and strait-laced freeze.

Brook become great from melted snows
Wears a g-string of ice to tease
And sequined, river's last chemise
Undone in a shudder goes.
The world is taking off her clothes.

One A.M. with Voices

Hers: What do you squander night for
       In coupling on a page
       Rhymes no man pronounces?
       Is it love or rage?
       The crouched cat pounces dream-mice,
       True mice play blindman's buff.
       For God's sake give the thing a pitch!
       I've lain cold long enough.

His: Did I write rhymes for love, sweet mouse,
       Then I'd have taken instead
       A sheaf of verses to my thighs,
       And rage—that's rape indeed.
       You are the single love I have.
       Be still. A further rhyme
       Plays cat-and-mouse about my head—
       Just a few minutes. I'm
       A mouser that must hurt awake
       With a green eye that roams:
       A shivering candle I must bear
       Where shapes twitch in dark rooms.

Hers: More endless rooms, old creeping tom,
       Than light can overtake.
       When did you ever catch a mouse
       But lean ones, wide awake?
       The plump drop to the hunter
       Who gropes them out when blind—
       How can you keep an eye on
       Every mousehole of the mind?
       Put cat and light out. You shall have
       The warmed side of the bed
       That sleep may with a breath blow out
       This guttering in your head.

Growing into Love (1969)

Cross Ties

Out walking ties left over from a track
Where nothing travels now but rust and grass,
I could take stock in something that would pass
Bearing down Hell-bent from behind my back:
A thing to sidestep or go down before,
Far-off, indifferent as that curfew's wail
The evening wind flings like a sack of mail
Or close-up as the moon whose headbeam stirs
A flock of cloud to make tracks. Down to strafe
Bristle-backed grass a hawk falls—there's a screech
Like steel wrenched taut till severed. Out of reach
Or else beneath desiring, I go safe,
Walk on, tensed for a leap, unreconciled
To a dark void all kindness.
                      When I spill
The salt I throw the devil some and, still,
I let them sprinkle water on my child.

Poets

> *These people are quenched . . . I mean the natives.*
> D. H. Lawrence, letter of 14 August 1923
> from Dover, New Jersey

> *Le vierge, le vivace, et le bel aujourd'hui . . .*

What were they like as schoolboys? Long on themes
    And short of wind, perpetually outclassed,
    Breaking their glasses, always chosen last
When everyone was sorted out in teams,

Moody, a little dull, the kind that squirmed
    At hurt cats, shrank from touching cracked-up birds,
    With all but plain girls at a loss for words,
Having to ask to have their fishhooks wormed,

Snuffers of candles every priest thought nice,
    Quenchers of their own wicks, their eyes cast down
    And smoldering. In Dover, my home town,
No winter passed but we had swans in ice,

Birds of their quill: so beautiful, so dumb,
    They'd let a window glaze around their feet,
    Not seeing through their dreams till time to eat.
A fireman with a blowtorch had to come

Thaw the dopes loose. Sun-silvered, plumes aflap,
    Weren't they grand, though? Not that you'd notice it,
    Crawling along a ladder, getting bit,
Numb to the bone, enduring all their crap.

Nothing in Heaven Functions As It Ought

Nothing in Heaven functions as it ought:
Peter's bifocals, blindly sat on, crack;
His gates lurch wide with the cackle of a cock,
Not turn with a hush of gold as Milton had thought;
Gangs of the martyred innocents keep huffing
The nimbus off the Venerable Bede
Like that of an old dandelion gone to seed,
And the beatific choir keeps breaking up, coughing.

But Hell, sleek Hell hath no freewheeling part:
None takes his own sweet time, none quickens pace.
Ask anyone, *How come you here, poor heart?*—
And he will slot a quarter through his face,
You'll hear a little click, a tear will start,
Imprinted with an abstract of his case.

Creation Morning

Needing nothing, not lonely nor bored,
Why should He have let there be light?
We can only guess: a pool
Turns us so tranquil a face
That, unsettled, we take up a stone
To shatter that placidness.

Could it have been what boys know
At the rim of a new-laid sidewalk
That for empty blocks extends
Like the smooth crest of the moon
Until the point of a stick
Drags the hand in its wake?—

What he knows who beholds in his bride
Only her willingness,
He placing clothes on a chair,
She lying on one white side
With an imminent look?
That may have been how it was.

Who would not start growth rings
Breaking on shores of bark
At the toss of a seed like a stone,
Though not an eye look on
In that time nor in any time,
Though in the solid dark?

Traveler's Warnings

Main Road West

The Late Late Show, rebounding from a hill
That screens the hangdog town, gives up its ghost:
A screen star ancient as this Oak Motel
Undergoes facelifts—loses voice—is lost
As the channel slithers from the set's blunt hook.
No magazines. No book but the Good Book.

Half-parted drapes, latched lock, and a long drink
In a glass meant for water. Almost gone,
Trees that grow leaves, as if you'd crossed a brink.
The wind's turned off, the sign USED CARS still on
That keeps hard stars from piercing through to town,
As though stars can be forsworn, or stared down.

Edgar's Story

What we'd been missing out on all those years
Of stoking up the coffeepot at dawn,
Those Sundays sitting working on some beers
Watching the sprinkler going on the lawn,
Was what we wanted. Gassed the old tin can
And lit out up the turnpike, Nell and I,
Soon as I got my fourteen-karat pen
And pencil set, and wrote, and it went dry.

Freight cars sat idling, rundown towns in tow.
Woods were the good part: straight up, all their boughs
Creaking with leaves. But then we'd have to go
Gawk at some china plates and pottery cows
Or snake farms where you stood and looked at snakes.
Now all those plastic squirrels that say, *I'm nuts
For the Dakota Bad Lands* on their butts,
That no one laughs at long, give me cold shakes.

Somehow out there with not much else around
In the motel at night, it starts to hurt,
Thinking—and your head beginning to pound
In time to the steady drip-dry of your shirt—
Of redwood forests melted down for pulp.
It ties a knot in my bowels
Each time I cost a branch to take a crap
And dry my hands off on some paper towels.

At Mount Rushmore I looked up into one
Of those faces born joined to the same neck bone.
I said, *Abe, Abe, how does it feel to be up there?*—
And that rock he has for a pupil budged, I swear,
And he looked me in the eye and he said, *Alone.*

National Shrine

Sanctioned by eagles, this house. Here they'd met,
Undone their swordbelts, smoked awhile and posed
Gazes that could not triumph or forget
And held their jowls set till a shutter closed.

Kentucky rifle now and Parrot gun
Cohabit under glass. Connecticut
And Alabama, waxed sleek in the sun,
Reflect like sisters in the parking lot.

Lee's troops led home to gutted field and farm
Mules barely stumbling. Borne off in each car,
The wounded sun and instant Kodachrome
Render our truces brighter than they are.

Peace and Plenty

Bound to the road by chains
Of motels, hills of pines
Under the moon lie stunned.
An Adirondack stirs

Winds, groping for her firs.
Engines are gunned

And, not knowing which path to choose
Through the chemical plant, the river
Choked with refuse
Upturns a blithering stare
To the exhausted air.
Crows hover.

Let the new fallen snow
Before she change her mind
Lay bare her body to the Presto-Blo,
The drooped rose her
Quietus find
Head down inside the in-sink waste disposer.

Driving Cross-country

Jack Giantkiller took and struck
    His harp and stalks sat up, all ears—
With wavelengths, corn in Keokuk
    Comes on so hard it interferes.

Glass empty in the Stoplight Lounge,
    Expecting to be stood a meal,
Ella Ashhauler has to scrounge,
    Her bosom tilted, for some heel.

A room the same as last night's room,
    Same brand of bath mat underfoot,
In thrall to some unlucky charm,
    We hurtle onward yet stay put.

Print of a bowling-ball-eyed child
    Broods on a sink of pseudo-pewter.

A wand's been waved, the whole house styled
    To offend no one, by computer.

Where is that prince of yesteryear
    Beneath whose lip princesses roused?
Bourbon will add a gleam of cheer.
    The place has lately been deloused.

When, headlight-blind, we let fall head
    On pillows hard by right-hand lanes
In airconditioned gingerbread,
    It keeps on driving through our veins,

Some hag's black broth. At dawn we stare,
    Locked into lane by rule of lime.
We had a home. It was somewhere.
    We were there once upon a time.

Reading Trip

> *Everybody's in po biz.*
> Louis Simpson

Just past a grove whose roots in overthrow
    Work air for nothing and boughs lie, still clung
With oranges stopped short, the towers show,
    Slim exhalations from a plastic lung,
        Shimmering faintly: knowledge reared with pride.
        Whose Hell is here? Nutt's letter for my guide,

I ask the straight way to the English Dep't
    Of girls too beautiful ever to be of use,
Wondering by what husbandry they're kept
    Golden and round, aburst with squeezing juice.
        The secretary, withered on her bough,
        Unclicks a gate latch. *"Mister Nutt's yours now."*

A handshake, hearty, fingers a little stiff
    From years of etching grades on freshmanese,
A pool-cue-following eye, though. Kind as if
    I'd been John Clare or one of the Trustees.
        Miss Cone will Beatrice me to the hall.
        God bless them, there'll be liquor after all.

With buzzer Nutt involves his teaching bard
    Whose class has just let out, who gropes at length
For the right gambit, picking his key word.
    He's read me, I've read him. Testing his strength,
        Each circles each, protecting his behind,
        Not knowing, sniffing after his own kind.

I'm in his hands for—what? a temperance lunch
    With all our eyebeams stuck fast to our plates?

With namecards, with the Tuesday-Thursday bunch
    Mulling the phases of the moon of Yeats?
        Jerusalem set free! He knows a bar
        For hot corned beef! *"Come on, I've got a car."*

And there in the click and hush of shuffleboard,
    Bridging our distances with pitcher-beer,
Something not far from sour truth being poured,
    Each makes out what the other has to bear.
        Close as a pair of long-lost concubines,
        We drink up, and misquote each other's lines.

After I'm let to stop off at the john
    It's time to do my poet act, the house
A thin third filled and looking put upon,
    Except for one attentive-as-a-mouse
        Pale braided lass with twitching button nose.
        Nutt shoos 'em down to fill the front-line rows.

I offer Hardy's "Ruined Maid," on watch
    For hints of acquiescence. About half
Coolly endure, let out their yawns a notch;
    Some look about—are they supposed to laugh?
        But here and there, a grin unprepossessed
        Glimmers, a lump of ore that's passed its test.

Then after, the popcorn-burst of handclaps spent,
    Will some hang on? Why, sure as Hell, released,
A few struggle forward, bold or hesitant,
    The better to read the fine print on the beast.
        Pale Mouse steals up on tiptoe and I'm slipped
        A morsel of her own mauve manuscript.

"How do you get ideas to write about?"
    I fumble for the old stuffed-owl replies:
Oh, I don't know, I guess I just start out

With a few words that match. *"What market buys*
   Poems about water sports?" My shoulders sag.
"Don't you find rhyming everything a drag?"

A drag, man? Worse than that. Between the eyes,
   I take the blade of his outrageous stare.
Whoever crosses him, the varlet dies,
    Trapped Guest to his unancient Mariner:
      "Get with it, baby, what you want to be
      So artsy-craftsy for? Screw prosody,

"Turn it on, man. It's like for now, today,
   Disposable stuff, word-Kleenex. Why take pains
Trimming it neat? Nobody gonna play
    That *game no more."* A man worth crossing brains
      And drinking up with, wrestling with all night—
      But not tonight, man. Let me off tonight.

The bard reprieves me. Soon there's clinking ice
   And bourbon in suburbia, a haze
Of settled evening. Out of artifice,
    Sated with me and all my works and days,
      I guess what drove one Welsh bard wild to squeeze
      Buttock and bottle. Miss Cone cuts blue cheese.

And here in this kindly orchard of the blest,
   Whose pretext for a stiff drink I have been,
This tenured, literate Oktoberfest
    That even paid to let me make its scene,
      Earth, it appears, will be bare earth indeed
      When they're chopped down, the last ones left who read.

Recloistered in the dry cell of my car,
   Ego discharging back to natural size,
I grope for balance, break off and discard
    Like petals of an artichoke, the lies

I stick out with all over, fumbling for
A means to shrivel back to a solid core,

Edge out into the dusk to claim my slot
In homeward-droning traffic, less and less
The bard on fire, more one now with the blot
That hoods the stars above Los Angeles,
Hard gunning, on the make for far-off nights,
Like any other pair of downcast brights.

Requiem in Hoboken

Their wives and children, spiffed up fit to kill,
Take front seats for the breaking of the crust,
Choir hums the Miserere, china saints
From Barclay Street look wide-eyed as though lost.
The celebrant, among chrysanthemums
Brought just a wink before the Bird with bread
Whistled straight off our heavenly Father's fist,
Moves threshingly in black to twist the Host,
Taste the raised wine. Peace fall upon those men
Of Hoboken the 5:11 train
Suddenly cut to lengths to fit the dust.

Wardheelers put up what the funeral cost,
But how can the grandest resurrection ever
Assemble their scattered bodies one by one,
Warm up the nestful till they hatch in Heaven
Without their thirsting at the very throne
For Guinness's (one free round every seven)?
Though graves give in like wharves weight's overgrown,
Lord, if you've got no hardboiled eggs to crack
On a marble bar, they'll bitch to be sent back.
The Bird broods on a setting of brown stone.

For a Maiden Lady

A tremor in her wrist
Forbade us to exist.
Fevers arose to burn
Her few twigs. All concern
Run past, her look congealed
Like a spare boudoir sealed
Upon the gilt snuff box,
Lavengro, the lace clocks
She had crocheted when able,
The postcard on the table,
Nasturtiums still dew-damp,
The stopped moth by the lamp,
All we who had played kind
So much dust thrust from mind.

Pottery Class

On Wednesday nights, the children rinsed and stacked,
The wives, their husbands closeted with *Time*,
From Lexington and Concord motor in
To travail in the elemental slime.

Thwack! and a hunk of muck hung by the heels
Has its back slapped, its breathing made to come.
Great casseroles take place on groaning wheels.
A vase commences, vast as Christendom.

Women, what's eating you? What is it drives
Your hands to forage, take up earth to knit?
Dull flickswitch chores? The drag of being wives?
The deep grave that a birth leaves after it?

Lay waste your manicures now though you may,
Yours is that furious core man stands outside,
Looking on helpless while you firm his clay
And bask him in your kilns until he's dried.

Absentminded Bartender

He'd meant to scare her, just, not hurt.
Who would have thought so light a tap . . .
Hey, you asleep?
                    He gave a start,
Cut off head dribbling from the tap.

Since then the cities and hotels
Had made one endless corridor
Of bulbs, extinguishers. Somewhere else
Was where he hung out more and more,
And drinking, though it made days worse,
Blurred how it had been, looking back,
And made time harder to reverse
Unless he had an egg to crack
And burst the yolk of. In his room,
Sunlight locked out, there sought for ease
In fresh positions legs and arms
Severed, alive, in bed with his.

Loose Woman

Someone who well knew how she'd toss her chin
    Passing the firehouse oglers, at their taunt,
    Let it be flung up higher than she'd want,
Just held fast by a little hinge of skin.
Two boys come from the river kicked a thatch
    Of underbrush and stopped. One wrecked a pair
    Of sneakers blundering into her hair
And that day made a different sort of catch.

Her next-best talent—setting tongues to buzz—
    Lasts longer than her best. It still occurs
    To wonder had she been our fault or hers
And had she loved him. Who the bastard was,
Though long they asked and notebooked round about
    And turned up not a few who would have known
    That white inch where her neck met shoulderbone
Was one thing more we never did find out.

Ant Trap

Innocuous as a clock, giving off whiffs
Of roast beef rare and bathtubfuls of gin
Free to the rank and file of working stiffs,
This Siren in a tin can lures them in.
A skull-and-crossbones on her lid warns men
Not to crack up against her reefs,
But how could that turn back an ant, his skin
Already bone, to whom death's head is life's?

Out through her punctured doors, down winding roads,
Each totes the backpack of his poison home
As an ex-GI remembers pallid broads
Who'd stand in wait beside Napoleon's Tomb
Beckoning with fingers and perfume.
He'd strike a bargain, never ask her age—
How you gonna keep 'em down on the farm
Or in a cubicle in some brokerage?

Not that the load he lugged home was the clap,
Although it might have been, nor yet the can
Of Spanish fly that good Rotarian
Smuggled back home to storm some woman's lap,
No dirtybook, no head cut from a Jap
Scrubbed to a whitened skull, but a slow campaign
Advancing, an inexorable malaise
To invade, subdue, and occupy his days.

And now, an insect marching in straight files,
In perfect press, his jawbone razored sleek,
He hops the same train daily, shuttling miles
To and from Montauk, hearing the same rails click,
Delivered nightly back to his Blest Isles,
Feeling his nerves go slack,

Greeting his wife with formulaic smile,
Sipping his scotch and soda, dazed, in shock.

Comparisons will fail. But guess how all
That army shuttling through it in a train
With nothing but its sweetness on one brain
Must feel when, home, their heartbeats falter and stall,
When, clutching sides, they double up in pain,
Loosen their footholds and begin to fall,
Cast forth weak feelers, grope, catch fast again,
Stiffening columns in behind a wall.

West Somerville, Mass.

1   Day Seven

Sundays we wake to tumbrels: iron wheels
Crack pebbles as they mount through Somerville's
Evasive sunshine. Round our blinded room,
From wall to wall reverberations drum.
Our newsboy with his railway baggage cart
Toils Medford Hill, up past the bleeding heart
Of the saint stuck in Apicelli's lawn,
Bearing the fat white body of the *Globe*
That comes in sections like a sacred robe,
Swearing as if he had it in for dawn.

The boy's breath coarsens, torn forth from his ribs.
They're sitting up now, crowing in their cribs.
Throwing things. I quit my sleeping wife,
Fumble tied shoestrings—O Lord, for a knife!—
Raise broken blinds, let daylight trickle through.
What was it, once, I used to have to do?
This day means beef not ground, the unmade dollar,
This day means Mutt and Jeff will come in color.
Time to feed ducks stale crusts, time off from pressure.
I trigger shave-cream from its can. Let's raze.
Deep in the mirror I confront two eyes
Like the last remaining windowpanes in blocks
Doomed for renewal, so far spared kids' rocks.

2   The Ascent

The rock rolled back, the stained race hatched out new,
They pass my window, the communicants
Each with two neat knife-edges in his pants.
In bathrobe still, out of it as a Jew,

Wonder Bread toast, cold coffee in my teeth,
My pencil marks time on a villanelle
That will not rise. Lord knows, up Medford Hill
I'd go too, but stop short before that wraith

My body risen, back, the old hale fellow,
All the same hangnails, chilblains, the whole bit,
Arms out for soul to re-embrace with it.
He'd be hard tack to swallow,

And, feet fast rotting, how to toe the line
On Mary's hoist to Heaven? Call it myth,
But that's pale stuff to slake a body with,
Water after Pope John's wine.

My faith copped out. Who was it pulled that heist?
Wasn't it me, too stuck-up and aloof
To spill my sins? If knocked on for a roof,
I wouldn't have a chair to offer Christ,

But He'd no more halt at my door than they
Unless to frown in on my snotty kids
Aping their bonnets, sporting potty lids.
One dark duenna screws up lips to slay

Me with a word. Peace, Momma!—I'd go back
To forehead ashes, giving up for Lent,
But gave up every blessed sacrament.
Can the strait gate still stand open a crack?

Who'd grudge joy to an angel, if it can?
Last night in the bathtub, groping for the soap,
I tried a sloppy act of love, felt hope
Batter my heart with vague wings. Pregnant man,

What's eating you? Good Friday, on to plunge
His lance, a soldier steps up, drives in hard,
Jeers and draws back. The captain of the guard
Offers a vinegar-soaked sponge.

Eventual as spring some goodman begs
The Body, decks it out in his own tomb,
Limbs in clean linen, wounds touched with sweet balm.
It happened while I shopped for Easter eggs.

O lukewarm spew, you!—stir yourself and boil
Or be not chosen. Strike with your whole weight
At hook, line, sinker—be fished or cut bait.
Give or get off the pot.

My boy steps up. He bites the loosening ear
Of his milk chocolate rabbit. Limb from limb
The victim's rendered. Let us eat of him
Some other year.

Each dawn the children rout me out. What profit
To shrink back like a dumb bulb? At a loss,
I stretch forth arms, fix feet as on a cross
Till something says, *Come off it.*

3   Golgotha

1968

Grey fur collars on a steel limb,
The welders, keeping warm
Inside their sheet-plastic cocoon,
Weave the new dorm
Late into night, deadlined
For April. According to plan,
The chewed hill's to be redefined
And seedlings, to a man,
Stood up in ranks to face blight,

Green lawn unrolled,
Brick walls adolescently bright
Sprayed to look old.

In my locked childproof basement work room
Furnace vapors
Chase their own tails. Roof-high, loom
Ungraded papers.
An iron door in a brick wall
A kick might splinter
Dikes back the ashes of all
Our hearths of winter.
I half-hear the thrash of bed sheets,
A mouse scratch, taking chances.
Down the spine of my dogeared John Keats
Mildew advances.

Cramped handwriting, don't know his name:
How Youth Is Shafted
by Society—now I've pegged him.
They got him. Drafted.
(Through vines in a gnarled neutral zone,
A locust nation,
Flamethrowers grazing, moves on
At its task, defoliation.)
Interesting idea, says my pen
To a John Bircher—liar, liar!
Shots rattle. No, the stuffed lion's
Brass eyeballs in the dryer.

I take out trash, not to read more—
Torn gift wraps, Christmas-tree rain—
Lift can cover on a white horde
Writhing. Lean rain
Blown to bits by the murderous wind
Has it in for you, finger and face,

Drives through every path to your brain,
Taking over the place
As though it had been here before,
Had come back in its own hour,
Snow gaining ground in the dark yard,
The mad in absolute power.

Ode

Old tumbrel rolling with me till I die,
Divided face I'm hung with hindside-to,
How can a peace be drawn between us, who
    Never see eye to eye?

Why, when it seems I speak straight from the heart
Most solemn thought, do you too have to speak,
Let out a horselaugh, whistle as I break
    The news to Mother that I must depart?

Moon always waxing full, barrage balloon,
Vesuvius upside down, dual rump roast,
Cave of the winds, my Mississippi coast,
    Cyclops forever picking up and chucking stone,

Caboose, poor ass I'm saddled with from birth,
Without your act, the dirty deed I share,
How could the stuck-up spirit in me bear
    Coming back down to earth?

Two Apparitions

1
Half in dream, half with me, she lay, some foal
    Barely born. As I crossed her spine
With a hand, out to join it and bind her stole
    Another man's hand, not mine,

A scaled hand, a lizard's, blotched over with bile,
    Every knuckle a knot on a stick
And in her cheek, dug there, a crone's wan smile.
    I shuddered. Wild-eyed she woke,

Then in the next moment the moon's white rise
    Cast the two of us smooth once more
And we fell to each other with tender cries,
    Backs turned on what lies in store.

2
Where no man laid eyes,
Down our bedroom wall
Slid the head of the moon
Like a genital
Hardly able to rise,
Too cold to assuage
Having had to look on
In diseased old age.

Artificer

Blessing his handiwork, his drawbridge closed,
    He sabbathed on a hill of hand-tooled wax.
On stainless steel chrysanthemums there posed
    Little gold bees with twist-keys in their backs.

Nothing could budge in this his country. Lewd
    Leaves could go slither other people's hills.
    His thrushes had tin whistles in their bills,
His oaks bore pewter acorns that unscrewed.

Increase perfection! So he shaped a wife,
    Pleated the fabric of her chartered thigh,
Begot sons by exact strokes of a knife
    In camphorwood. He told them not to die.

The moment flowed, as did his cellophane
    Brook over rollers. All obdurate day
    His player-piano tunkled him its lay,
Though on its ivory dentures a profane

Tarnish kept ripening, and where the tide
    Slid on ballbearings ceaselessly to shore,
Red rust. All night the world he'd locked outside
    Kept thrusting newborn rats under his door.

Daughter in the House

This sleeping face, not even mine nor yours,
A hard thing to have charge of, not to own,
Settled on us through time as ocean floors
Bestow them in long snowfalls made of bone:
A face half foreign, half of some we know,
Borne down upon her as a gem occurs
Out of the first leaves ever tree let go
From tons that crushed dead faces into hers.

Smooth as the skin upon a pail of cream,
Her sleep hides ferment. Would we work her wrong
To lift it off and peer in on her dream?
Hasn't she been down in herself too long?
But no—two pools abused by thunderbursts,
We regain balance in her quiet spells.
She is our drink. It was for her our thirsts
Singled out each other's wells.

The Shorter View

Her eyes outstretched from seeing how in space
Stars in old age will stagger, drop, and burst,
Throwing out far their darknesses and dust,
My wife lets her book fall with stricken face.
She'd thought tomorrow set and rooted here,
And children. That some morning will occur
Without a sunrise hadn't dawned on her.
Kathleen some great pink shell held to her ear,
And wistful, staring through me to an earth
Littered with ashes, too dried-up to bear—
Though I say what the hell, we won't be there—
She doesn't see much point in giving birth
And in our dark bed where her burden grew,
When I'd make love and recklessly let live,
Her arms drawn shut, tonight she will not give
One inch of ground for any shorter view.

Giving in to You

Laird of a makeshift castle,
My drawbridge tugged up tight,
I sat supplanting light,
Hard striving to be facile.

I wrote a book. It dried,
I stood it on my shelf
And feasted, pride
A mouth swallowing the body from around itself.

But now I give in to you
As the house of the county poor's
Gauze curtains do
To the luxurious wind
That knows how to be kind,
That overflows all outdoors.

Slim Volumes

Breaking and Entering (1971)
Emily Dickinson in Southern California (1973)
Celebrations After the Death of John Brennan (1974)
Three Tenors, One Vehicle (1975)

Breaking and Entering (1971)

Song: Great Chain of Being

Drinking smooth wine in a castle or digging potatoes knee-deep
    in dung,
Everybody in creation knew just how high or how low he hung
On that ladder with Lord God at the top, dumb mud at the bottom
    rung,
            Great Chain of Being,
            Great Chain of Being.

Well, man was top dog on Mother Earth and woman was his
    marrow bone
And a woman giving suck to a child cut more ice than a woman
    alone
And the cruddiest of sparrows glittered more than any precious
    stone
            In hierarchy,
            In hierarchy.

Then Copernicus picked up his hammer, Galileo held the spike,
And they hit that Great Chain a wallop just as pretty as you like—
Old Earth went flying from her center like the sprocket out of a
    bike,
            All its spokes busted,
            All its spokes busted.

Nowadays every critter goes rattling around, worked loose from
    that golden chain
And the angleworm and the angel can't connect with each other
    again
And me, I'm fixing to let myself play out in the pouring rain,
            Snapped off and dangling,
            Snapped off and dangling.

Now I wonder who's been sitting in the Good Lord's old arm chair,
I wonder if there's still snakes down below and a Blessed Mother
   up there
Keeping an eye on me or just the credit bureau and Medicare—
         Is *seeing believing?*
         Is *seeing believing?*

Consumer's Report

> *They don't make things like they used to.*
> American proverb

At meat, or hearing you deplore
    How soon things break, my mind salutes
John Dowd, who'd bring by rolling store
Horse radish to our kitchen door
    He'd made from cream and home-ground roots.

Good God, the heat of it would burn
    Right through your beef and knock your tongue out.
Once, for a snowsuit I'd outgrown
Came so much free stuff in return
    It smoldered down and ended flung out.

Why did he wear that look of pain
    Strangely, although his trade kept thriving?
They say the fumes get to your brain.
One day he came round with a cane
    And someone else to do the driving,

But ground right on with open eyes
    And, grinding, stared straight at his killer.
I bet theirs takes them by surprise
Though they can see, today-type guys,
    The guys who use white turnip filler.

The Atheist's Stigmata

Good Friday eve, the nail holes in my wrists
And ankles pop like bubbles. Doctor, feel
This opening in my side—put your hand there—
People reach out to me. Why can't I heal
Those babies' scabs like helmets? Can't forget
By drinking—only the gradual rounding-out
Of buds in April warmth helps. Less and less
I feel a pain too godly to express.
My back works loose from invisible planks.
A thief again and not the Middle Man
Till next year. Father, I'd be forsaken, thanks.

In a Secret Field

Stealthily
the snow's soft tons

by the air
unbearable

accumulate.

Emily Dickinson in Southern California (1973)

Mining Town

Sheds for machines that lower tons of men
Hug dirt for dear life. Clapboard houses lose
Clapboards the way a dying oak sheds bark.
One house they tell of plunged
Nose-down into a shaft last year with cries
Of sleepers waking, falling.

Like boys in sneakers testing limber ice,
Gas stations growing bold now inch up near.
Who recollects that Kitchen Kounter World
Straddles Pit One? Dull coal-oil-colored clouds
Graze to the west.

Born in this town, you learn to sleep on edge,
Always on edge, to grow up like a tree
Locked to the wind's sharp angle. When fear tells
It tells out of the corner of an eye,
A rickety house balancing in uncertainty.

Schizophrenic Girl

Having crept forth this far,
So close your breath casts moisture on the pane,
Your eyes blank lenses opening part way
To the dead moon moth fixed with pins of rain,
Why do you hover here,
A swimmer not quite surfaced, inches down,
Fluttering water, making up her mind
To breathe, or drown?

All autumn long, earth deepening its slant
Back from the level sun, you wouldn't quit
That straitbacked chair they'd dress you in. You'd sit,
Petrified fire, casting your frozen glare,
Not swallowing, refusing to concede
There are such things as spoons. And so they'd feed
You through a vein
Cracked open like a lake to icefish in—
Can no one goad
You out into the unsteady hearthlight of the sane?

Already, yawning child
At some dull drawn-out adult affair,
You whimper for permission to retire
To your right room where black
T-squares of shadows lie, vacuity
A sheet drawn halfway back.

If you'd just cry. Involved
Around some fixed point we can't see, you whirl
In a perpetual free-fall.
Hear us. We cannot stand
To see turned into stone what had been hand,
What had been mind smoothed to a hard steel ball.

Evening Tide

Darkness invades the shallows of the street.
A tricycle left outdoors starts nodding and bobbing.

On his recliner by dusk set afloat
Father's head lolls, his dome of beer half-emptied.

Under the parked car in the driveway, shadows seep,
And from somewhere the cry of a child protesting bed
Comes blundering in again and again, a stick of driftwood.

A Little Night Music

Fingers untwist the taut
Peg of a thighbone, chin
Takes hold, bow draws a light
Test cry from violin.

In love we tune for death,
So if you're not averse,
My dear, undress. In bed
We'll dress-rehearse the hearse.

Celebrations After the Death of John Brennan (1974)

1
What do they praise, those friends of his who leap
Into a frenzied joy since Brennan died
By his own rifle in his mother's house
Along a rock road on a mountainside?
Do they bring gong and incense, do they stage
Some egocentric homemade Buddhist Mass?
Word halts me as I'm climbing Medford Hill,
Poor East Coast Rocky, ice still in its grass.

I hold on to a railing, drag my steps
Up stepping-planks. Two lines he'd written stare:
Why is it *celebrations often seem*
Contrived as war?

2
Churned by the wind, the iceberg of his death
Slowly revolves, a huge stage without act.
A seat bangs like a gunshot, pushbrooms sweep
Littering paper: poems, scribbled chords
For his guitar. Days earlier he'd climbed
To East Hall, where the literati live,
And had me get a load of one last song.
Could I have swerved him from his blackout phase?
Could anyone? For many must have sensed
A furious desperation in his gaiety.
Chance not to grieve dissolving moons—
An ashen grin of craters on the wane
Emerges and submerges in green waves.

3
Forever looking freshly tumbled out
Of a haystack he'd shacked up in, cockeyed grin
Disarming as a swift kick in the chin,
He had a way that put pretense to rout.

That was one hell of an opening
Pedagogue-student conference—
Cracking rot-gut red in his dorm pad
Till we basked in dippy glows,
Reading aloud his latest hundred poems:
Fragments of mirror ranged along a strand
For the sun to rise on, overflow, expose.

4
Teachers and shrinks had pestered him to vow
He'd walk in straight lines—John the circler-by
And lazy wheeler? *Does your infinity
start sooner than mine?* How could he die
From no more than a quarrel with a friend
Or lovers' falling-out?
                    Yet he'd backpacked
His death collapsed, a hiker's metal cup
In readiness. He'd seen it clear: each poem
A last note scribbled in a hand that shook
I'd been too blind to read. An aftermath
Of snow clings to the Hill,
Betrays the path.

5
Dissolved, those fugitive songs
Blown out of mind: breath from a halted lung
As though a burst of rain had stricken away
Bright beaded webs the dew had hardly strung.

6
Home from his Sligo ramble, John toiled nights
Tooling his pen-and-inks, photographs, words,
Self-published his tombstone
In that one cryptic book
And like Huck Finn attended his own rites.

I break it open. Now its message stares,
Plain, that back then had seemed half rained away.
His lens had gorged on thorns, worn timbers, chains,
A ruined abbey, stonework walls a loss,
Where a surviving gunslot window yields
A partial view of a constricted cross,
Black children peering through an iron gate—
columbines grow well in boulderfields.

7

Gowned as a clown with greasepaint tears drawn on,
John wraps stunned Seymour Simches six times round
With monkey rope, binding them both together,
Falls on his prat. We bystanders implode
With silent laughter.

I don't aspire to be your father, John.
I only tried to copyread your words.
You and my own blood sons, let you break free
From mentors, from long-tied umbilical cords.

8

"Well, most of me's still here," my old man said
After the surgeon pared him, still bright-eyed,
Needing no son's rash sword where three roads meet,
At eighty-eight as guileless as a child
Right to the end. John gone. Which one was wise,
An innocent grown old or a wizened boy?
To cling to life with fingerless right hand
Or, with a twitch of a finger, blow it away?

9

Far from your Rockies, John, did you find home,
Second home on the gaunt cliffs of Moher
Whose face held hide-outs from the Black and Tans,
Men perched in grottoes, cawing out to sea?

Climbing those crags, did you defy the gale,
Dreaming, a scrap of turf grass in your fist,
Your long look swooping in an arc to trace
The coastline of a gull?

10
Shank end of spring. A night held in his name.
A full throng waxes. Thin forsythia
Of Medford thrusts indifferent sprigs again.
No prayers, no introductions, no plan,
Yet each knows when to rise and speak in turn,
To do a simple dance, sing, or read lines,
When to join arms, to circle and return.
Nothing's decreed and yet all present know
The clockstroke when the celebration ends.
Red wine stands lower in its gallon jug,
The night grows bright, reluctant to grow late.
It is John Brennan, not John Brennan's death
We celebrate.

Three Tenors, One Vehicle (1975)

Talking Dust Bowl Blues

Old cow's almost dry now, her hooves scrape hard dirt.
Where's the man going to pay me what I'm worth?
Forty acres played out, soil like the corn meal low in the can
Reminds me of a woman holding back on a man.
Nights, hot nights I walk by the warped board fence
Hoping to find some fresh water breakthrough or some sense.
Seeing my kids wear nothing but washed-out flour bags
Makes my heart move like a man with one lame foot that drags,
Packing 'em off to bed before sundown every night
So they won't run around and work up an appetite,
Hearing 'em whine in the dark through the bunk room door,
We only had nine stew beans, can't we have some more?
Had my fill of hanging around this town
Like a picture on a nail waiting to be took down.
Seen my name writ ten times on a yellow pad,
Don't mean a damn, they don't send for you, makes a man mad.
Stalk of corn can grub its roots deep, find iron in dry ground.
Let a man try, he can't go deep—where's food to be found?
Shoes wearing thin not from plowing, not from working a road,
Just from tromping, getting nowhere, carrying their same old load.
Beth used to wear her hair in a neat combed braid,
Now she lets it fall any old way down her forehead.
Black topsoil used to roll off from the eye straight north,
Nothing now but the wind towing dust clouds back and forth.
No point trying to make a living in this town.
Going to fix me an old Ford, lay them patched tires round and
    round,
Going to head due west where the oranges hang low,
Let my kids eat too, pick red pears right off of the bough,
Furry peach bending the branch, its stem thumb-thick,
Shrinking back from your hand like a young cunt from a prick.
Dust clouds bearing down now, stretching pole to pole.
No use staying here till I'm dried in the long dust bowl.

Song to the Tune of "Somebody Stole My Gal"

> *I'm fed up with people who say, Boo hoo,*
> *somebody stole my myths.*
> W. D. Snodgrass, in conversation

Somebody stole my myths,
Stole all their gists and piths.
Somebody pinched my Juno and Pan,
Crooked Dionysus
And caused my spiritual crisis.
Some no-good no-account
Made my centaur dismount.
Somebody in a laboratory coat with test-tube in hand
Mixed nitrogen with glycerin and poof! went my promised land,
    oh,
Hear me crying,
Don't much like forever dying.
Somebody stole my myths.

Cross Ties: Selected Poems (1985)

In a Dry Season

Willing to rise yet weighted down with thought,
I am that early would-be aeronaut
Who yearns to mount the clouds, but only walks,
Flapping upholstered arms, emitting squawks.

And why do I, who strive to straddle stars,
Settle for beers in dingy singles bars?
Descend, O Muse. Bestow, ungracious slattern.
Quit circling Boston in a holding pattern.

A Footpath Near Gethsemane

for Raymond Roseliep

Child: Mary, Mary, wan and weary,
        What does your garden grow?

Mother: Tenpenny nails and Veronica's veils
        And three ruddy trees in a row.

Dirty English Potatoes

Baildon, West Yorkshire

Steam-cleaned, so groundless you'd believe
    Them exhaled from some passing cloud,
The Idahoes and Maines arrive
    Same-sized, tied in a plastic shroud.

Their British kindred, unconfined,
    Differ in breeding, taste, and size.
They come with stones you mustn't mind.
    You have to dredge their claypit eyes.

Their brows look wrinkled with unease
    Like chilblain-sufferers in March.
No sanitized machines are these
    For changing sunlight into starch—

Yet the new world's impatient taint
    Sticks to my bones. I can't resist
Cursing my mucked-up sink. I want
    Unreal meals risen from sheer mist.

Goblet

from Hugo von Hofmannsthal, "Der Beiden"

Goblet in hand, she strode to him,
Her light chin level with its rim,
So quick her stride and she so skilled
At fetching, not a drop she spilled.

Steady as hers was his own hand
That drew his ripple-muscled colt
Shuddering to an abrupt halt
With a casual gesture of command—

Yet as he reached forth one hand
Almost to hers and would take hold,
The goblet seemed too huge to take.
Because the two of them so shook
Neither could find the other's hand.
Over the ground the dark wine rolled.

Aunt Rectita's Good Friday

Plate-scraping at the sink, she consecrates
To Christ her Lord the misery in her legs.
Tinges of spring engage the bulbous land.
Packets of dyestuff wait for Easter eggs.

Frail-boned, stooped low as she, forsythia
In its decrepitude still ventures flowers.
How can He die and common life go on?
A beer truck desecrates God's passionate hours.

He died for those who do not give a damn.
Brooding on sorrowful mysteries, she shoves
Into its clean white forehead-fat the ham's
Thorn crown of cloves.

Hangover Mass

Of all sins of the flesh, that reprobate
    My father had but one, and it had class:
To sip tea of a Sunday till so late
    We'd barely make it up to Drunkards' Mass.

After a sermon on the wiles of booze,
    The bread and wine transformed with decent haste,
Quickly the priest would drive us forth to graze
    Where among churchyard flocks I'd get a taste

Of chronic loneliness. Red-rimmed of eye,
    Quaking of hand, old men my old man knew
Would congregate to help bad time go by:
    Stout Denny Casey, gaunt Dan Donahue

Who'd mention girls with withering contempt,
    Each man long gone past hope to meet his match
Unless in what he drank all night, or dreamt.
    Each knee I stared at cried out for a patch.

A mere half-pint, I'd stand there keeping mum
    Till, bored to death, I'd throw a fit of shakes.
Then with relief we'd both go stepping home
    Over sidewalk cracks' imaginary snakes.

One-night Homecoming

Opening the door, he grasps my suitcase handle,
But can't quite lift it. Breathes hard, mounting stairs.
She doesn't notice yolk stuck to the dishes,
Nailheads arising from the kitchen chairs.

Where are the kids? In school. *You didn't bring them?*
I'm still your kid, I say, but can't compete
With her persistent needling iteration
That hurts without intending to, like sleet.

From my childhood bed I follow in the ceiling
The latest progress of each crack I know,
But still the general cave-in hangs suspended,
Its capillary action running slow,

And that thick roof I used to think unchanging
Creaks with the wind. It's my turn now to fall
Over strewn blocks, stuffed animals on staircases,
To read the handwriting crayoned on the wall.

October

Flat-tired, the year sets out red roadside flares.
    An olive football in a casual toss
    Ovals its chain of overthrows across
A wind-stirred dry martini. But the air's

As of two minds: to thunder or forgive?
    Clouds hold their fire. The parching widow's-bless
    Purses weak lips. Trees' signals of distress
Turn more flamboyantly demonstrative.

Were we two stout perennials at heart
    Who knows what light we'd make of time's abuse.
    Sleep near me. Be a tough nut to work loose
Before harsh hoarfrost wrenches us apart.

Joshua

Earth stopped. The Holy City hit a mountain
As a tray of dishes meets a swinging door.
Oceans lunged to converge one with another.
He who had called that halt stood bemused there.

Who would have thought a simple invocation . . . ?
Like brazen leaves, troops fell. His walking stick
Tapped as he limped across a foiled battalion.
Sun and moon hung stone still, their axles stuck.

No cricket sprang from upright walls of grass.
Clouds swung in bunches, birdless. Who could look
Long on so high a carnage: all creation
Crushed like a sprig of heather in a book?

Futile to wail, wear sackcloth, tear his tongue out—
How could he feel commensurate remorse?
As last the sun, God resting noncommittal,
Rose in confusion and resumed its course.

Old Men Pitching Horseshoes

Back in a yard where ringers groove a ditch,
These four in shirtsleeves congregate to pitch
Dirt-burnished missiles. With appraising eye,
One sizes up a peg, hoists and lets fly—
A clang resounds as though a smith had struck
Iron on an anvil. His first blow, out of luck,
Rattles in circles. Hitching up his face,
He swings, and weight once more inhabits space,
Tumbles as gently as a new-laid egg.
Extended metal arms surround their peg
Like one come home to greet a long-lost brother.
Shouts from one outpost, mutters from the other.

Now changing sides, each withered pitcher moves
As his considered dignity behooves
Down the worn path of earth where August flies
And sheaves of air in warm distortions rise,
To stand ground, fling, kick dust with all the force
Of shoes still hammered to a living horse.

To Dorothy on Her Exclusion
from *The Guinness Book of World Records*

Not being Breedlove, whose immortal skid
Bore him for six charmed miles on screeching brakes;
Not having whacked from Mieres to Madrid
The longest-running hoop; at ducks and drakes
The type whose stone drowns in a couple of skips
Even if pitty-pats be counted plinkers;
Smashing of face, but having launched no ships;
Not of a kidney with beer's foremost drinkers;

Fewer the namesakes that display your brand
Than Prout has little protons—yet you win
The world with just a peerless laugh. I stand
Stricken amazed: you merely settle chin
Into a casual fixture of your hand
And a uniqueness is, that hasn't been.

At the Last Rites for Two Hotrodders

Sheeted in steel, embedded face to face,
They idle now in feelingless embrace,
The only ones at last who had the nerve
To meet head-on, not chicken out and swerve.

Inseparable, in one closed car they roll
Down the stoned aisle and on out to a hole,
Wheeled by the losers: six of fledgling beard,
Black-jacketed and glum, who also steered
Toward absolute success with total pride,
But, inches from it, felt, and turned aside.

Flitting Flies

They come. No sooner do I lift
Eyelids on day than out they drift,
Invaders colorless as rain,
Dim spaceships made of cellophane.

Alert for signs of bad intent,
I watch. So far, benevolent.
What earthly purpose can they serve,
These vermin of the optic nerve?

Between my retina and light
They blur each page I read or write,
Squiggling their plumes, and slowly trace
Amorphous progresses through space.

When in the heat of puberty
Those vague May flies first rose in me,
I thought my hangdog soul abhorred
In the fierce eyeball of the Lord—

Took them for Limbo's brats let loose
To strike me blind for self-abuse
And in each ectoplasmic blot
Beheld some wraith I'd half begot.

Near autumn's climax now, I know
That in their escort I must go
To walk my last mile, vision blurred
Until it lights on one last word.

At least, from peering out through cells
I know that blindness to what dwells
Too far beyond or swarms too near
Is my best hope of seeing clear,

No longer certain there can be
Ideal fish of porphyry
Nor indiscriminately fond
Of lurkers deep in my own pond.

The Death of Professor Backwards

slain January 29, 1976

Three hard-eyed kids hot on a fix's heels,
Enraged at the cash he had, few bills and small,
Did in James Edmondson, famed vaudeville's
Professor Backwards. Three slugs through the skull
Closed his great act: the Gettysburg Address
About he'd switch and back-to-front deliver.
Transposed perfectly them at back hurl he'd
Out called crowd the in hecklers any whatever.

More than clashed glass in Vegas clubs fell still
That night his heart backpaddled to a stop:
Unheard lay songs that once with dazzling skill
His brainpan's funhouse mirror used to flop.
A listening Sennett, applause his to command,
Why had it to be him, so lean of purse,
Felled like a dog in an alley when his blind
Fate shot back like a truck parked in reverse
To hurl him backwards, trailing gory clouds?
The world will little note and long forget
How often watchers in whole spellbound crowds
Would light the wrong end of a cigarette.

At Brown Crane Pavilion

after Ts'ui Hao, about 800 A.D.

An old god-man rode off on his brown crane.
What's left behind? His dedicated shack.
Ten hundred years of white clouds wandered by.
Brown crane's long gone. Not likely he'll be back.

By river glow, each leaf sticks out its veins.
Parrot Island grass—oh, smell it! shed your shoes!
Sun knows its way down home. Wish I knew mine.
Got the mist on the river, waves on the river blues.

On the Proposed Seizure of Twelve Graves in a Colonial Cemetery

Word rustles round the burying-ground
Down path and pineconed byway:
The Commonwealth craves twelve heroes' graves
For a turn-lane in its highway.

Town meeting night, debate is slight.
Defenders of tradition
Twitter and cheep, too few to keep
The dead from fresh perdition.

With white-hot gaze emitting rays
Observes Selectman Earnwright,
"Some stupid corpse just wastes and warps
Where traffic needs to turn right!"

Embattled still within his hill,
One farmer loosed a snicker.
"When once ten redcoats dogged my arse,
I did not light out quicker

"Than when in a foss our scraps they'll toss
Therein to blend and nuzzle
Till God's last trump lift skull and rump,
One risen Chinese puzzle.

"Late yesterday as I listening lay
And the sweet rain kindly seeping,
I would have sworn I heard Gabe's horn
But 'twas rush-hour beeping.

"Upon my life, old Marth my wife
Will soon regret I chose her

When through our bosom-bones protrude
Posterity's bulldozer."

Rose a voice in wrath from under the path,
"Why skulk we in this cavern?
Come, lads, to arms!—as once we formed
One morn at good Fitch Tavern!

"Are we mild milksops nowadays?
Do not we still resemble
The men we were, for all Time's wear?
Collect your bones! Assemble!"

But the first wraith gave a scornful laugh.
"With muskets long outmoded?
We'd stuff the crows like corn you'd throw
Ere our poor barrels we loaded.

"For we dead," mused Seth, "but squander breath
On current ears. 'Tis plain
They'd amputate Christ's outstretched arms
To make a right-turn lane."

A Beardsley Moment

Adoze upon her vast aplomb,
    The tittering-stock of palace mice,
Lulled by the ticking of her bombe
    Of deliquescent orange ice,

Victoria forgets to reign—
    From slackening hand crochet-hook falls—
Oblivious though snails design
    Priapic doodads down the walls,

Though Dryads merge and Mignonette,
    Venereal hair a lilac bruise
Beneath drawers of lace fishing-net,
    Discards—plip, plop—her swansdown shoes

In bed, a plate. A satyr carves.
    Off in a corner, veiled from scorn,
Sly hoptoads with the heads of dwarves
    Fall on a whimpering unicorn,

Its wide eyes Albert's as a child.
    Now centaurs pearl-rope-draped in drag
Bear off the head of Oscar Wilde
    To Paris in a Gladstone bag.

Dark Horses (1992)

The Arm

A day like any natural summer day
Of hide-and-seek along the river shore
Till Snaker, probing with a snapped-off branch,
Dredged up a severed arm,
Let out a shout of glee
And shook it in my face like some grim charm.

In nightmares even now,
Dribbling dark bottom-ooze,
Those fingers green with algae, infantile,
Reach out to grapple me—
I spun and ran, abandoning my shoes,
Snaker and that little horror at my heels.

Was it a scrap of flesh
Or only rubber wrenched loose from some doll
Who died and bit the trash? I never knew,
But that it couldn't fasten on at will
Made sense. And so I tried
Not fearing it, tried all night long, but still

Night after night that arm
Joined to a wrinkled baby with no nose
And cratered eyes would tap my windowpane,
Its cries squeezed shrill from trying to break through:
Why do you leave me out here in the rain?
It's dark and cold. Let me come sleep with you.

Twelve Dead, Hundreds Homeless

The wind last night kept breaking into song—
Not a song, though, to comfort children by.
It picked up houses, flung them down awry,
Upended bridges, drove slow trees along
To walls.
         A note so high
Removed an ear that listened. On the strand
Without a word this morning, sailors land.
White cars, their sirens off, wade silently.

Now crews inch by, restringing power lines,
Plowing aside the sparkling drifts of glass.
The wind last night kept breaking into song
Beautiful only if you heard it wrong.

The Waterbury Cross

Autumn. You're driving 84 southwest.
A hillock scarlet as a side of beef
Accosts your eyes. Gigantic on its crest,
A cross stands outstretched, waiting for its thief.

Your fingers as if hammered to the wheel
Clench hard. Frost-kindled sumac blazes down
Like true gore pouring from a bogus crown.
The earth grows drizzled, dazzled, and bedrenched.

Did even Wallace Stevens at the last,
Having sown all his philosophe's wild oats,
Gape for the sacred wafer and clutch fast
To Mother Church's swaddling petticoats?

Connecticut's conversions stun. Is there
Still a pale Christ who clings to hope for me,
Who bides time in a cloud? Choking, my car
Walks over water, across to Danbury.

Veterinarian

Terrified bleat, bellow and hoofbeat, thrash,
She quiets with black bag. Working alone
On hands and knees, a carpenter of flesh,
She joins together staves of broken bone,
Mends fences for the bloodstream that would run
Out of the raving dog, the shattered horse,
Her hands as sure as planets in their course.

Now prestidigitates before the wide-
Eyed children without trying to, intent
On tugging forth a calf, live, from the bride
Of the bull, bandages the brood mare's ligament.
Now by her labor arteries are bent,
Grappled, tied fast. With one last firm caress,
She murmurs words to soothe the languageless.

Leaves like a plowman order in her wake.
Home for a hot tub and a lonely feast
Of last night's pizza, watching cold dawn break,
Knowing that some will live—a few, at least—
Though foam-jawed, wild-eyed, that eternal beast
Annihilation with perpetual neigh
Takes worlds like ours with water twice a day.

The Animals You Eat

The animals you eat
Leave footprints in your eyes.
You stare, four-year-old pools
Troubled. "They don't have souls,"
I tell you, in defeat.

Has no one ever dined
In bedtime stories pink
Cuddlable pigs inhabit,
No one stewed Peter Rabbit
In that land of pure mind?

You tinker with your burger,
Doubtful. "It doesn't matter,"
I say. We kill by proxy
And so, like Foxy Loxy,
Dissemble while we murder.

"Lambs wouldn't have a life
Romping in black-eyed Susans
If they weren't to be eaten."
But your lip quivers. Beaten,
I'm caught with dripping knife.

To bed now. Gravely wise,
You face night on your own.
I smooth your pillow and sheet.
The animals you eat
Start turning to your eyes.

Snug

What, dead? Aunt Edith, whom the children dubbed
    The Bug behind her back? Have her hands dropped
        That sheaf of metered mail
        She'd leaf through for real letters? Have her frail
    Clock-stockinged legs, now done with running, stopped?

How shall we do without her seasonal
    Flutter of air through rudiments of wings,
        Her stay announced for "at most fourteen days"
        (Oh, never less), her ladybirdlike ways
    Of scurry, scamper, scoot, of fondling things

In multifocaled insect spectacles?
    Preoccupied with faintly useful service—
        Polishing nutpicks, Wooliting toy lambs' fleece,
        Giving each pillowcase a sharper crease—
    She'd do her best to please. But make us nervous.

What care she'd spend on folding gently things,
    On children, creatures—questing, we now see,
        Some borrowed resting place, as beetles who,
        Needing some knot of comfort to undo,
    Couch in the center of a peony.

Can it be that near evening, after all,
    The earth begrudged her scurrying brief stay?
        Hardly. Inter The Bug
        In that prim chrome-clasped touring bag she'd lug
    When, wings part-warmed, she'd poise to skim away.

Overnight Pass

The front had such a rutted look
That on the move through hers
You seemed to ford streams, mount hills thick
And dark with tufted firs.

A lone bulb's eyeball by her bed
Lit roads in disrepair
Yet regiments came scatheless through
The barbed wire of her hair,

Up from her body's stony trench
Where many a private crept,
Ducked for a while the kiss of shell
And caught his breath and slept.

Two from Guillaume Apollinaire

1   Pont Mirabeau

Under Pont Mirabeau flows the Seine
      And loves of ours
    Must I think back to when
Joy followed always in the wake of pain

    Sound the hour   night draw near
    The days go running   I stay here

Hand in my hand stand by me face to face
      While underneath
    The bridge of our embrace
Weary of everlasting looks the slow waves pass

    Sound the hour   night draw near
    The days go running   I stay here

Love flows away as running waters went
      Love flows away
    As life is indolent
And Hope is   violent

    Sound the hour   night draw near
    The days go running   I stay here

Though days run on though days and weeks run on
      No time gone by
    Nor love comes back again
Under Pont Mirabeau flows the Seine

    Sound the hour   night draw near
    The days go running   I stay here

III

2 Churchbells (*Les Cloches*)

Gypsy tall dark my lover
Listen the churchbells sound
We loved each other and got lost
Not dreaming we'd be found

But we were badly covered up
Now every bell has spied
Our secret from its steepletop
And spilled it villagewide

Tomorrow Cyrien and Henri
Catherine and Marie Ursule
The baker's wife the baker
And Cousin Gertrude all

Will smile at me when I walk by
I won't know where to lay me
You'll be far from my side I'll cry
    And that will kill me maybe

To the Writers Forbidden to Write

In shadowland you learn to wear
A doublebreasted shadow suit,
A mask for when you venture out.
You sleep, flesh draped across a chair.

To stand up straight you have to bend.
You jump, your path crossed by a cat.
You start awake when telephones
Clang from the floor above your flat

As if the light of day might bring
The clocklike latch, unlatch of arms
While in a thousand basement rooms
Your thoughts explode like fire alarms.

Terse Elegy for J. V. Cunningham

Now Cunningham, who rhymed by fits and starts,
So loath to gush, most sensitive of hearts—
Else why so hard-forged a protective crust?—
Is brought down to the unresponding dust.
Though with a slash a Pomp's gut he could slit,
On his own work he worked his weaponed wit
And penned with patient skill and lore immense,
Prodigious mind, keen ear, rare common sense,
Only those words he could crush down no more
Like matter pressured to a dwarf star's core.
Let eyes unborn wake one day to esteem
His steady, baleful, solitary gleam.
Poets may come whose work more quickly strikes
Love, and yet—ah, who'll live to see his likes?

On Being Accused of Wit

Not so. I'm witless. Often in despair
At long-worked botches I must throw away,
A line or two worth keeping all too rare.
Blind chance not wit entices words to stay
And recognizing luck is artifice
That comes unlearned. The rest is taking pride
In daily labor. This and only this.
On keyboards sweat alone makes fingers glide.

Witless, that juggler rich in discipline
Who brought the Christchild all he had for gift,
Flat on his back with beatific grin
Keeping six slow-revolving balls aloft;
Witless, La Tour, that painter none too bright,
His draftsman's compass waiting in the wings,
Measuring how a lantern stages light
Until a dark room overflows with rings.

Emily Dickinson Leaves a Message to the World Now that Her Homestead in Amherst Has an Answering Machine

Because I could not stop for Breath
Past Altitudes – of Earth –
Upon a reel of Tape I leave
Directions to my Hearth –

For All who will not let me lie
Unruffled in escape –
Speak quickly – or I'll intercept
Your Message with – a Beep.

Though often I had dialed and rung
The Bastion of the Bee –
The Answer I had hungered for
Was seldom Home – to me –

The Withdrawn Gift

The homeless on the sidewalk said
As we walked by, *Wish I was dead?*

And sat back in his self-made pond
Of piss. Your eyes flashed, *Don't respond.*

And so the quarter in my hand
I'd meant to toss him didn't land.

Denying him, I felt denied
A swig from that brown-bagged bottle, pride.

On the Square

Circling the walk
Where rusty benches on scaled birdlegs perch,
Contending for one kernel, wings alurch,
     Two he-males stalk.

Neither will acquiesce.
A beak-tipped arrow, one dives for the other,
Grasps and tears off some neck-fluff. Whorls of feather
     Phosphoresce.

Slowly as though in dream,
The dealer in crack unjackknifes from his bench,
Twitches numb muscles, makes stiff fingers clench,
     A switchblade gleam

In his right hand, to sway
Over a huge-eyed boy. "You holdin' out
On me. You took in pretty near about
     Eight hundred, say?"

The hireling's shrugs default
His contract obligation. Straight down swings
The blade—its edge bites feelinglessly, slings
     Blood to asphalt.

Now like a wine-
Skin pierced the body in its outrush veers
To earth. The dealer pivots, disappears.
     A siren mourns.

The boy is let to lie
Mouth open, draining. Like a funeral barge
A stately stretcher comes. Nurse tugs her charge
     Home lest she testify.

      Meanwhile, at one remove,
From the cool eaves of the urinal
Plump hens with throats of umber, breasts of coral,
      Flute and approve.

Dump

The brink over which we pour
Odd items we can't find
Enough cubic inches to store
In house, in mind,

Is come to by a clamber
Up steep unsteady heights
Of beds without a dreamer
And lamps that no hand lights.

Here lie discarded hopes
That hard facts had to rout:
Umbrellas—naked spokes
By wind jerked inside-out,

Roof shingles bought on sale
That rotted on their roof,
Paintings eternally stale
That, hung, remained aloof,

Pink dolls with foreheads crushed,
Eyes petrified in sleep.
We cast off with a crash
What gives us pain to keep.

As we turn now to return
To our lightened living room,
The acrid smell of trash
Arises like perfume.

Maneuvering steep stairs
Of bedsprings to our car,
We stumble on homecanned pears
Grown poisonous in their jar

And nearly gash an ankle
Against a shard of glass.
Our emptiness may rankle,
But soon it too will pass.

Summer Children

These summer children, quickly made
In marriages that came undone,
Exchange tin shovels. Up from sand
They palm-press walls against the waves.
What currents do they understand?

Like creaking-pulley gulls, they quarrel —
They've taken too much sun today.
Now foam consumes their castle keep,
Draping their towels with sodden laurel.
Children, it's high time. Come away.

Concussions of the surf resound
As though in shells. Once sunken deep,
Like driftwood a September chill
Rises, returns. From summers gone,
These children may be all we keep.

Tableau Intime

The thin-chinned girl diagnosed as hyperactive
Curls in a heap on the couch, limp from the rebuke
Of her large mother who stands imploring, "Practice,
Damn you, practice your violin." A stream of puke

Pours from her mother's live-in lover's lips
Into the toilet crock at which he kneels,
A penitent communicant. Froth drips,
Spins down the drain. His feet regained, he wheels

Back to the parlor, balances the couch
With his slumped weight. Cora kicks off her shoes,
Seizes the cheap, neglected violin,
Scrapes out a dissonance. "Can't hold your booze?"

She jeers. The lover eyes her with disdain,
Aims a sharp swing but misses. "Ma!" she shrills,
"Ma, stop him! Fritz is hitting me again—
He's always hitting me." "Time for your pills,"

Calls Mother, reappearing with two bottles,
Capsules for Cora, Four Roses straight for Fritz.
Stunned by a bounding shoe, in its waterless bowl
The paint-mottled pet turtle collects its wits.

Finis

Like an ice swan, the party melts. It's late.
Karen calls names, Blanche falls to yanking hair.
Wadded and blown through straws, the cake in bullets
Splatters, grape Kool-Aid puddles every chair,
Fudge sauce eats through each sodden paper plate.

Vision begins to shimmer—are you dreaming?
Like a tired child impatient parents drag
Out to the car, you're strongarmed, all your winnings
Clutched in a little sequined paper bag.
It's cold. It's growing dark. You go off screaming.

Black Velvet Art

On a corner in rain-riddled Lewiston blooms a stand
Of giant paintings, guaranteed made by hand:
Elvis with hairdo laced with bright gold nimbus,
Jesus with heart afire, arms wide to bless
Your pickup truck, a leopard crouched to leap
Upon a bathing beauty sound asleep,
And all resplendent on a jet-deep back-
Ground of profoundly interstellar black,
Blacker than deepest space,
So that these cat-toothed colors spring to deface
Eyes disbelieving.
                    Gaseous scrimmages
Of car and bus gun by these images
That blossom where the Androscoggin flows
Between banks that sprout work socks and cheap shoes,
Where old men hark back to that glory day
When Liston took a dive for Cassius Clay.

That corner glimmers still, a world apart
From this one. Two-for-fifteen-dollar art
Fulfills a need not known, for which we yearn
Unwittingly. The next day we return
To find all wonder banished,
The pavement gray and blank, its gallery vanished
Like stars at that final dawn when God commands
Even the last black hole, *Get off My Hands.*

The Lords of Misrule (2002)

"The Purpose of Time Is to Prevent Everything from Happening at Once"

Suppose your life a folded telescope
Durationless, collapsed in just a flash
As from your mother's womb you, bawling, drop
Into a nursing home. Suppose you crash
Your car, your marriage, toddler laying waste
A field of daisies, schoolkid, zit-faced teen
With lover zipping up your pants in haste
Hearing your parents' tread downstairs—all one.

Einstein was right. That would be too intense.
You need a chance to preen, to give a dull
Recital before an indifferent audience
Too kind to jeer you and too slow in clapping.
Time takes its time unraveling. But, still,
You'll wonder when your life ends: Huh? what happened?

Jimmy Harlow

My third-best friend in fourth grade, Jimmy Harlow,
Like some shy twitch-nosed rabbit
Yearning to quit its burrow,
By teacher's harsh words once brought down to tears—
That day when, nine, you charged across the street
Not reckoning the car you'd meet by chance,
You stained the blanket thrown
To keep the snowflakes from your broken bones
And whined there, waiting for the ambulance.

After that accident
You lived just four more years,
Your skull crushed oblong, frail,
Face ashen-pale
And graven with an ineradicable squint.
I saw you last
At a New Year's party, locked in fierce embrace
With the loveliest girl in the place,
Dredging her with your sharp-chinned corpse-gray head.
I was aghast.
By April you were dead.

Lie in the ease of winter, Jimmy Harlow.
If I begrudged you her, I do not now.

Naomi Trimmer

Young, you aspired. Coloratura soprano,
Blossoming voice, you might have been the rage
But for that moment on the concert stage
When fright struck. Hearing your cue repeat,
You croaked one raucus note, then turned and ran
In tears while your accompanist's piano
Pronounced a benediction on your slain
Career. A silence like a gale through wheat

Tore through the house. You crept back home, quite mad,
Then lived alone. In bizarre homemade gowns
Of multicolored calico you'd flounce
Along our main street, curtsy to my dad,
Pee in the gutter daintily, demand
Your same seat at the dime-store lunch each noon,
Arriving not one second late or soon.
If someone had usurped your place, you'd stand

Muttering till he fled. Your room was cold,
You'd complain, shrilling, "I demand attention!"
Your janitor stood staring, mouth agape
At stacked sheet music luminous with mold,
Boas of fur, a mildewed opera cape—
He gazed with deepening incomprehension
Upon those relics of your long-closed show
And all your windows flung wide to the snow.

In memory you stride with lunatic smile,
Chin-chucks that triggered children's howls, immense
Frowsy rose-freighted hats, pink parasol,
Faint bows to an invisible audience.

You stalked our streets for decades till the blaze
Consumed your crumbling rooming house and caught
The fringes of your robe. And then our days
Grew colorless. A nuisance gone, some thought.

Five-and-Dime, Late Thirties

Your nose by frying franks'
    Salt pungent odor stung,
You'd perch on a stool, give thanks
    For shreds of turkey strung

On a mound of stuffing doled
    With ice-cream scoop, lone spoon
Of gray canned peas, one cold
    Roll, cranberry half-moon.

The same recorded air
    Swung round the counters daily:
Once more, "Old Rocking Chair"
    Had captured Mildred Bailey.

Inclined, some lone gray head
    Lost in a dream apart
Selecting glasses, read
    With slow lips from a chart.

Rouge-cheeked, a queenly jade
    In permanent spit curls
Pushed Maybelline eye shade
    To adolescent girls.

At times a beaten bell
    Insistent as Big Ben
Proclaimed the news: some swell
    Had tried to change a ten.

On to the thick cheap pads
    With your last dime to blow,
To write fresh Iliads
    You'd steer course, even though

You longed for chocolates
    From the open-air glass case
Where, nightly, hordes of rats
    Shat in the licorice lace

Until one day the Board
    Of Health padlocked the door.
As sure as FDR
    Had kept us out of war,

Brown Shirts were just a show,
    Hitler a comic wraith
Far off. What you don't know
    Won't hurt had been our faith.

Sailors with the Clap

Slumped against bulwarks in the corridor
Beside the door to Sick Bay, they await
Their morning needle-jabs and running sore
Inspections, four who stayed ashore too late.
Deflecting with a bitter grin the taunts
Of passersby, each man smokes thoughtfully,
Counting his shots, his daily penances,
Like beads told on a cast iron rosary.

Faithful as monks to rule, they to routine.
Dreading the engines' constant homeward drives,
Daily they pray, *Dear Lord, don't let our wives*
Meet us until we once again come clean.
At sea, even Benedict or Alcuin
Might envy them their chastely ordered lives.

For Allen Ginsberg

Ginsberg, Ginsberg, burning bright,
Taunter of the ultra right,
What blink of the Buddha's eye
Chose the day for you to die?

Queer pied piper, howling wild,
Mantra-minded flower child,
Queen of Maytime, misrule's lord,
Bawling, *Drop out! All aboard!*

Foe of fascist, bane of bomb,
Finger-cymbaled, chanting *Om*,
Proper poets' thorn-in-side,
Turner of a whole time's tide,

Who can fill your sloppy shoes?
What a catch for Death. We lose
Glee and sweetness, freaky light,
Ginsberg, Ginsberg, burning bright.

Thebes: In the Robber Village

"They're lice!" declares our archeologist
Turned tour-guide, grinding out his cigarette.
He steps on it with furious heel twist. "Why
Aren't the scum rich? I'll tell you. Every one
Of them's an addict. Heroin comes high,
Because when caught a pusher has to die.
Let's move. It's bloody hot here in the sun."

He hates them for positioning mud huts
Over sealed tombs. By night they burrow down
To salvage golden combs and jars of coin,
A hawk-beaked granite Horus, angry eyed,
An alabaster Bes, that scowling dwarf,
Protector of the pregnant, or a ring
That, held to light, reflects a heron's wing.

Winking at them with cameras, we stroll,
Pursued by urchins. One thin barefoot girl
Nibbles from empty fingers. Given cash,
She yells—and we're surrounded in a flash
By babbling kids. A watchful tourist cop
Comes swooping down to stop
Our brief careers
As Francises and Clares,
Scatters the rabble, saves us and the day
With upthrust club. We make our getaway.

Our archeologist insists, in sore distress,
That henceforth we take vows of selfishness.

Close Call

How suddenly she roused my ardor,
That woman with wide-open car door
Who with a certain languid Sapphic
Grace into brisk rush-hour traffic
Stepped casually. I tromped the brake,
Her lips shaped softly, "My mistake"—
Then for a moment as I glided
By, our glances coincided
And I drove off, whole ribcage filled
With joy at having not quite killed.

Street Moths

Just old enough to smoke but not to drink,
    Grown boys at night before the games arcade
Wearing tattoos that wash off in the sink
    Accelerate vain efforts to get laid.

Parading in formation past them, short
    Skirts and tight jeans pretending not to see
This pack of starving wolves who pay them court
    Turn noses up at cries of agony—

Baby, let's do it! Each suggestion falls
    Dead to the gutter to be swept aside
Like some presumptuous bug that hits brick walls,
    Rating a mere *Get lost* and death-ray eyes.

Still they go on, in blundering campaigns,
    Trying their wings once more in hopeless flight,
Blind moths drumming the wires of windowscreens.
    Anything. Anything for a fix of light.

Décor

This funky pizza parlor decks its walls
    With family portraits some descendant junked,
Ornately framed, the scrap from dealers' hauls,
    Their names and all who cherished them defunct.

These pallid ladies in strict corsets locked,
    These gentlemen in yokes of celluloid—
What are they now? Poor human cuckoo clocks,
    Fixed faces doomed to hang and look annoyed

While down they stare in helpless resignation
    From painted backdrops—waterfalls and trees—
On blue-jeaned lovers making assignation
    Over a pepperoni double cheese.

The Ballad of Fenimore Woolson and Henry James

I
Constance Fenimore Woolson,
Expatriate of middling years,
Had to tilt back her head to listen
Through the keener of her shell-pink ears.

Uncle Jim had conceived Leatherstocking,
But a thorough bluestocking was she
And her novels of artist heroines
Set her free to a life fancy free.

Women writers, she knew, in retired shade grew
While the sun shone on male scribes' names;
Still, a glimmer of admiration grew
Between Fenimore and Henry James.

Now a feelingful hat-tilt from Henry
Might have ended her loneliness,
But Henry was wedded already, it seemed,
To his ethical consciousness.

Down the twilit Strand, not quite hand in hand,
Folded handkerchiefs on their wrists,
They would sidestep drunks and Victorian punks
And the placards of anarchists.

On a steam train chugging to Stonehenge,
Inquired Fenimore, "Were you a druid,
Henry, would your granite dagger
Scatter my vital fluid?"

"Why," said Henry, "you obstinate pagan!
Do you crave such a primitive feast?

I'd not have a clue whom to sacrifice you to,
For an artist's his own high priest."

2
One evening as Fenimore went strolling
Past Hyde Park, rioting mobs
Of the hungry were halting the hansom cabs,
Planting kisses on duchesses' gobs.

Fenimore's heart beat faster
To see such outrages occur.
She walked a while wistfully after the mob,
But nobody halted her.

In her Florentine villa Henry
Came to stay under Fenimore's roof
Where he, although ever considerate,
Kept distinctly a bit aloof.

Wrote Fenimore, "Mr. James is coldish,
With a brown beard, taller than John Hay,
And a beautiful regular profile,
Large expressionless eyes, light gray.

"Mr. James would infiltrate me
With his own sense of the past.
He insists I admire the Duomo
But I find it too cold and vast.

"Insufficiently acquainted
With nude torsos, flanks, and the lot,
I can't tell the supremely beautiful
From bare bottoms that are not."

Oh, they'd drive their pens every morning,
Cappuccino for fuel. With sighs,

Each would labor over a love scene,
Take a lunch break, then revise.

The wily old cook who attended them
With brandy breath and prescient leer,
Would bring Henry notes from Fenimore—
Gesù Cristo, these Inglèsi were queer!

3
Henry fled. He wrote back to Fenimore
Deft sentiments out of his heart
Signed "faithfully," which, as the weeks went by,
Came noticeably farther apart.

In a Dolomite Alp inn, Fenimore
Stared out across masses of snow
In her flimsy chemise, a mere ten degrees
Below out. Where now to go?

In a palace in Venice, Fenimore
Came down with a feverish flu.
She turned and tossed, figured all was lost,
And she knew what she needed to do.

At midnight she made up a pretext
To dispatch the nurse from her room
And in nightdress stole from her sickbed
For a sudden blind date with doom.

She lurched to the open casement,
Flung her left leg over the sill,
Crying, "Lord, if you're watching forgive me,
But the sum of my life is nil.

"I shall join the eternal mountains,
Be an object of beauty, and then

Have no more to do with the sorrow
And despair of women and men."

Two passersby kicked at a bundle
Of white cloth that uttered moans.
It was Fenimore, leaking her life away
On the cold-nosed cobblestones.

Back in London, Henry at high tea
Accepted a wire with the word.
He added a spoonful of sugar
Though the first he had not yet stirred.

He slowly walked down Great Ormond Street,
He lifted his gaze to the air,
Asking, "Tell me, my sensibility,
What there aught of which I wasn't aware?"

But the air, uncomprehending,
Kept silent all the while
Although he had tendered his question
In his earlier lucid style.

4
Sifting Fenimore's papers, Henry
Came on letters in his own hand
On which with speed he set flames to feed
Lest anyone misunderstand,

Yet a trace of her fragrance lingered
And a subtle unspoken yes
As those yellowing pages rustled
Like a never-worn wedding dress.

Swept away by an urge to wipe out
Every last stitch that had been hers,

He gathered like sheaves at harvest
Her camisoles and stomachers,

And, conveyed under stealthy moonlight
By Tito, his gondolier pal,
He consigned that enormous bundle
To the deeps of the Grand Canal,

But around his craft—was he going daft?—
There arose in the fog and fetor
A flotilla of domes, each round as Rome's
Basilica of Saint Peter,

For before his eyes a phenomenon
Had emerged from that dank lagoon:
Each billowing gown he had tried to drown
Blown up like a black balloon.

Henry gaped aghast. The accusing past
From out of the darkness surged—
Then the gondolier's pole poked a puncturing hole
And each ghost with a sigh submerged.

5
Henry had a dream: he was running
Through a jungle in furious haste—
Muffled footfalls drew near, drew steadily near,
And the breath of an unseen beast.

In Rome, at the Protestant Cemetery,
Henry rang at the wrought iron gate,
Sent in visiting card and ascertained
That his stickpin was stuck in straight.

"Who's there?" whispered Fenimore, rising,
"Who's making that terrible din?"

She took one glance at his visiting card
And sent word she wasn't in.

Henry kept on standing and standing.
Why, there must be some hideous mistake.
Above him a lowering storm cloud
Relinquished a lonesome flake.

He slipped through the gate and beheld it:
The plot where she now dwelled apart,
Where a pride of stray cats came prowling
For a morsel of Shelley's heart,

Where the broth of the brawling empire
Seethed under its cloud-cover lid
And time had transformed to silver
The absurd old Pyramid

And her newly placed cross. He would fling him
Like a whipped dog across her grave!
Yet as he drew ready to do so
He knew that such a gesture would save.

Henry went back to his writing desk,
Spread paper like an open chart
And he drew dear Fenimore into his arms
And transformed her to a work of art,
Still living,
Transformed her to a work of art.

A Scandal in the Suburbs

We had to have him put away,
For what if he'd grown vicious?
To play faith healer, give away
Stale bread and stinking fishes!
His soapbox preaching set the tongues
Of all the neighbors going.
Odd stuff: how lilies never spin
And birds don't bother sowing.
Why, bums were coming to the door—
His pockets had no bottom—
And then—the foot-wash from that whore!
We signed. They came and got him.

To His Lover, That She Be Not Overdressed

And why take ye thought for raiment?
Matthew 6:28

The lilies of the field
    That neither toil nor spin
Stand dazzlingly revealed
    In not a thing but skin

And in that radiant state
    Sheer essences they wear.
Take heed, my fashion plate.
    Be so arrayed. Go bare.

The Blessing of the Bikes

> *The pastor of St. Daniel's Church in Lyncourt, N.Y., held*
> *his annual "blessing of the bikes" ceremony yesterday*
> *in the church parking lot. More than 400 motorcyclists*
> *attend the spring rite, which signifies the start of the riding*
> *season.*
> AP news item

It's that morning of mornings in April
When the mockingbirds oil up and sing,
So I yank snakeskin pants on at dawning,
Head for church, engine going *ka-jing.*

There's suburbans with high-boughten karma
In their kangaroo-fur safety suits,
Even, revving a Ducati Darmah,
A couple of gray-headed coots;

There are Hell's Angels studded and goggled
Under helmets with steeple-top spikes—
All the bunch of us mounted and clinging
To those old rugged crosses, our bikes.

So I elbow my hog a bit closer
And Monsignor he solemnly takes
Up his sprinkler of blest holy water
And bestows us a couple of shakes,

Then he mutters some magic in Latin
Asking Jesus to pull a few wires
That'll sure-fire prevent our damnation
Should the treads ever peel off our tires.

So my pimple-faced skinny old lady
Jumps aboard with her shuddering crotch

Crushed up next to my butt while I kick off
And ease up to speed notch by notch.

Well, we're off like a clean whoosh of whaleshit.
Oh, we're one nasty beast, one mean boat.
I wind open the throttle in second
And an anthem growls out of its throat.

Bitter road-dust and rattle of pebbles,
Bugs we eat—nothing matters a damn,
For the spring air soars by, consecrated
By the blessing of I AM WHO I AM.

Superhuman, I peer through black plastic,
Passing Jags like they're nothing but wrecks,
For the Virgin is perched on my handlebars
Keeping watch on our breakable necks.

Sharing the Score

All through *Don Giovanni* the lovers hold
The cumbersome score between them like a chart
To orchid-spattered islands drenched in storms,
Their fingers moving to the music's pace,
Tracking libretto, skimming note and bar
As, naked, they might trace each other's forms.

Coughs from the curtained boxes, whispered words
Cannot distract this pair from their pursuit
Of paradise. Out of a fast-food bag
They share cold wurst. An orchard brewing fruit,
A paper harp to play glissandi on,
The score ordains the downfall of the Don.

To Mozart's mind, love hallows quenchless thirst.
Turning each page, intent, their fingers glance.
At last Don Pedro's stone shape rumbles in
To ask, "Is dinner ready yet?" Accurst
Hot hands yank Giovanni down to Hell
And passion hurls them off to their hotel.

A Curse on a Thief

Paul Dempster had a handsome tackle box
In which he'd stored up gems for twenty years:
Hooks marvelously sharp, ingenious lures
Jointed to look alive. He went to Fox

Lake, placed it on his dock, went in and poured
Himself a frosty Coors, returned to find
Some craven sneak had stolen in behind
His back and crooked his entire treasure hoard.

Bad cess upon the bastard! May the bass
He catches with Paul Dempster's pilfered gear
Jump from his creel, make haste for his bare rear,
And, fins outthrust, slide up his underpass.

May each ill-gotten catfish in his pan
Sizzle his lips and peel away the skin.
May every perch his pilfered lines reel in
Oblige him to spend decades on the can.

May he be made to munch a pickerel raw,
Its steely eyes fixed on him as he chews,
Choking on every bite, while metal screws
Inexorably lock his lower jaw,

And having eaten, may he be transformed
Into a bass himself, with gills and scales,
A stupid gasper that a hook impales.
In Hell's hot griddle may he be well warmed

And served with shots of lava-on-the-rocks
To shrieking imps indifferent to his moans
Who'll rend his flesh and pick apart his bones,
Poor fish who hooked Paul Dempster's tackle box.

Pie

Whoever dined in this café before us
Took just a forkful of his cherry pie.
We sit with it between us. Let it lie
Until the overworked waitperson comes
To pick it up and brush away the crumbs.

You look at it, I look at it, I stare
At you. You do not look at me at all.
Somewhere, a crash as unwashed dishes fall.
The clatter of a dropped knife splits the air.
Second-hand smoke infiltrates everywhere.

Your fingers clench the handle of a cup
A stranger drained. I almost catch your eye
For a split second. The abandoned pie
Squats on its plate before us, seeping red
Like a thing not yet altogether dead.

Shriveled Meditation

On junkyard hills the flattened frames
    Of cars that failed to veer
Mount to the sky like damage claims,
    More massive every year.

Long raised, hitchhikers' wistful thumbs
    Lie level with the wind.
Leaves lose their grip. The earth becomes
    Increasingly thick-skinned.

State secrets that don't dare survive
    Pour through the greedy shredder
And I and everyone alive
    Go right on going deader.

Meditation in the Bedroom of General Francisco Franco

Life is a short night in a bad hotel.
St. Teresa of Avila

Behind an oak door triple-locked
    And those few soldiers he could trust
To stand with firearm hammers cocked
    He slept the sweet sleep of the just

While motionless there lay within
    A reliquary by his side
The left hand of Avila's saint,
    In life discalced, now calcified.

How could he think that all his dreams
    Of foes consigned to abrupt rest
By firing squads and torture teams
    Her gracious fingers might have blessed?

What if, one dark night while he slept,
    That hand had stolen from its crypt,
Shedding brown flakes, and slowly crept
    Over his well-oiled closely clipped

Mustaches, over lips that hissed,
    Down past each pouch of facial suet
To fasten on his throat and twist?
    Teresa, you had your chance. You blew it.

Maples in January

for Edgar Bowers

By gust and gale brought down to this
    Simplicity, they stand unleaved
    And momentarily reprieved
From preening photosynthesis.

Abandoned, tons of greenery
    As though scorched bare by forest fire,
    They've shrugged the rustle of desire,
The chore of being scenery,

And now impervious to thirst,
    No longer thrall to summer's sway,
    They stand their ground as if to say,
Winter and wind, come do your worst.

September Twelfth, 2001

Two caught on film who hurtle
from the eighty-second floor,
choosing between a fireball
and to jump holding hands,

aren't us. I wake beside you,
stretch, scratch, taste the air,
the incredible joy of coffee
and the morning light.

Alive, we open eyelids
on our pitful share of time,
we bubbles rising and bursting
in a boiling pot.

New Poems

Panic in the Carwash

In neutral, hunched down worried at the wheel,
I'm trundled through a claustrophobic cave
Of swatting fingers, brushes, gushes, thrown
Back to the womb, suspended on a chain,
Helpless while hands perfect me in the dark.

Christ, let me out! Release me, get me born
With eyes unfinished, anything to see
This waterfall of wax drip to a stop,
These obstetricians halt. Bring on, bring on
That sweet green light at uterus's end,
Roll me into the sunlight, whack my back.

At Paestum

Our bus maintains a distance-runner's pace.
      Lurching on tires scraped bare as marrowbones,
It hauls us past a teeming marketplace.
      We shun life. What we're after is old stones.

Pillars the Greeks erected with a crane
      Went up in sections as canned fruit is stacked.
An accurate spear could pierce a soldier's brain
      Before he'd even known he'd been attacked.

Bright fresco of a wild symposium
      With busy whores, nude boys, a choice of wines—
("And where in Massachusetts are you from?")
      Abruptly, snowdrifts clasp the Apennines.

"Wouldn't you think him practically alive?"
      Says someone of a youth fresh out of school
Painted upon a tomb, who makes a dive
      Into the next world's waiting swimmingpool.

Lunch is a belch-fest: rigatoni, beer.
      A sawtoothed wind slices through flat-topped pines.
Weathered white temple columns linger here
      Like gods who went away and left their spines.

Rites

a Mesolithic burial at Vedbaek, Denmark

I drew my first and last breath by her side,
The one who bore me and in bearing died.

They placed her on a couch of leaves, beneath
Her head spring blossoms, shells of snail, deer teeth,

And so that I who stopped here might fly on,
They made my bed the spread wing of a swan.

Small House Torn Down To Build a Larger

Because it squatted on a piece of land
Whose cash price overtook and dwarfed its own,
Its owner couldn't stand to let it stand,
But sold it to be stripped to vein and bone.
That mottled bathroom sink where hair was brushed
Until its drain grew maddeningly slow,
That toilet tank so difficult to flush,
The closet floor on which the cat would go
Are rubble now. Acerbic histories
That ended in divorce, the hopeful past
Sprawl with extracted nails and toppled trees,
Too little in the living room to last.

Uncertain Burial

Under Ben Bulben's shadow
Your bones serenely lie,
Dark limestone cut as you decreed,
Cast a cold eye,
If your own bones for certain—
More likely, a jumbled toss
Of some pauper's skull and ribcage
Into a common foss.
That abbé of Roquebrune
Who threw you away perhaps
Considered your phases of the moon
And gyre-spins worthless scraps.
When redfaced French officials
Hastily combed the mound,
Proclaiming all your fragments
Indubitably found,
What traveled home by warship
With public pomp and show
To lie in Drumcliff churchyard?
How can it matter now
Whose ribs and dental fillings
To Ireland had been shipped?
No coffin lid's your ceiling.
Though flesh from bone be stripped
Like veils of gossamer,
Your words stay hard and whole:
Nails driven into the bole
Of your great-rooted blossomer.

Innocent Times

When doctors puffed their cigarettes and fat
    Advanced unchecked, invading hordes of hearts,
When cheap thermometer and thermostat
    Leaked jets of mercury like poison darts,
When every shoe store's miracle machine
    X-rayed cramped bones within ill-fitting shoes,
When like a knight in armor Listerine
    Slew dragon Halitosis, clear heads chose
Calvert, and loving housewives loaded pies
    With sugar (as "your family deserves"),
When soothing syrup smothered babies' cries
    And Sanka vanquished Mister Coffee Nerves,
When toothpaste came in squooshy tubes of lead,
    And safety belts in cars seemed passing fads,
How in the Sam Hill could you end up dead?
    Hadn't you lived according to the ads?

Epiphany

On the whale-watch boat from Gloucester
As waves kept striking, pitching again their tents,
Somebody shrieked—one monstrous fullmoon eye
Protruded from the water
As if some phantom, homing from that time
When a squirrel might course
Across tree crowns and branches never touching
Earth from the Cumberland to the Mississippi,
Had risen out of the deep
To ogle us, accusing.

Furnished Rental

Brief tenants of a beachfront house
    Battered by winds but built to last,
We jigsaw puzzle solvers piece
    Together fragments of its past

From snapshot albums, pictures framed—
    Somebody's wedding on the pier
With wide-eyed flower girls costumed
    In silks like foam from sea or beer—

Dried starfish, outcasts of a storm,
    Abandoned hats we don for laughs,
The son in Army uniform
    Absent from later photographs.

That locked and shuttered room left dark—
    Does it hold things they won't bequeath:
China we'd break, clocks stopped to mark
    The moment of some cradle death?

Sailboats approaching out of mists,
    Their summers haunt us. From their story
We armchair archeologists
    Infer our own *memento mori.*

Brotherhood

Hungry at dawn, anointing slabs of bread
With oily peanut butter, I remember
The snare I'd laid. Perhaps a mouse and I
Share the same menu?

I kneel and from beneath the sink retrieve
The sprung trap, in its clasp
The forehead of a victim who'd believed
Its prize within his grasp.

Stiff frozen tail, expression of chagrin—
Into the trash compactor. Dust to dust.
It owes me nothing more, this guillotine
Sprung many times, blood-stained, springs red with rust.

Thoughtful, I chew a half-stale apple tart.
More tempting baits I've risked my neck for, but
When will that ring of fat around my heart
Snap shut?

Death of a Window Washer

He dropped the way you'd slam an obstinate sash,
His split belt like a shade unrolling, flapping.
Forgotten on his account, the mindless copying
Machine ran scores of memos no one wanted.
Heads stared from every floor, noon traffic halted
As though transformed to stone. Cops sealed the block
With sawhorse barricades, laid canvas cover.
Nuns crossed themselves, flies went on being alive,
A broker counted ten shares sold as five,
And by coincidence a digital clock
Stopped in front of a second it couldn't leap over.

Struck wordless by his tumble from the sky
To their feet, two lovers held fast to each other
Uttering cries. But he had made no cry.
He'd made the city pause briefly to suffer
His taking ample room for once. In rather
A tedious while the rinsed street, left to dry,
Unlatched its gates that passersby might pass.
Why did he live and die? His legacy
Is mute: one final gleaming pane of glass.

Pacifier

her night thoughts

My baby wails. That I may rest,
I thrust him rubber knob, not breast,
And soon like waves by oil suppressed

He calms. An underhanded trick,
Placebo quick and politic.
He cries for bread, I give him brick,

But when night circles round to four
I'll open to him like a door
And give him all he wants and more.

As old wives say, it may be true
That love delayed can still accrue.
Sometimes give only part of you.

Your lover's tide may rise in flood
When there's no answer in your blood—
Then let that raging bull chew cud

And drop to sleep. Let him return
When in coincidence you burn.
Fire lingers near a kindled urn

And lives to rage again, and spreads
On real as on imagined beds
Held fast by things that stand in steads.

Geometry

They say who play at blindman's buff
    And strive to fathom space
That a straight line drawn long enough
    Regains its starting place
And that two lines laid parallel
    That neither stop nor swerve
At last will meet, for, strange to tell,
    Space throws them both a curve.

That theory lets my hopes abide,
    For even though you spurn
My love and cast me from your side,
    Yet one day I'll return;
And though we coldly part, to run
    Our separate ways, a tether
Shall join our paths till time be done
    And we two come together.

Silent Cell Phones

In airport waiting rooms, owners of cell phones
Look wistful when their phones lie silent, millstones
That no stream turns. Mindful of their high stations,
They squirm and fidget their exasperations,
Prisoners staring at a blank cell wall,
Their fingers idle on each speechless phone.
There ought to be a number they could call
To demonstrate to us they're not alone.

Fireflies

for A. M. Juster

Concupiscent, the fireflies cruise
    Our twilit lawn. They stay out late
Blinking their signs to advertise
    STUD WANTED and *BRIGHT MALE SEEKS MATE*.

With intermittent lust they blaze
    Just for a fortnight's fling, as if
Their code were fixed: Enjoy your days,
    Die young and leave a handsome stiff.

One temptress sucks a tourist in
    With counterfeit come-hither flashes
Like those of females of his kin,
    But in her jaws his hopes turn ashes.

Somehow their incandescent dance
    Obscures our dark view of the dark's
Enormity as they advance
    By graceful swoops that end in sparks.

Complacently, we watch them glow
    Like kindly lantern lights that sift
Through palm fronds in Guantanamo
    On the torture squad's night shift.

Mrs. Filbert's Golden Quarters

Seven pounds of poems
undone, half-done, undoable
sit stalled in a box
margarine came in.

All these itsy-bitsy piddles,
puddles, piffles,
trifles, fizzles, etc.
ache like turds
stuck in my chute.

O Missus Filbert,
get thee to a creamery.
Got to utter
butter instead
of golden quarter-dead
words, toss stale stuff to the birds,
bake fresh bread.

Jerry Christmas

Strutting and serpenting the one wide street
In Skibbereen, County Cork,
Pie-eyed on stout, you pipered a parade
Of prancing little kids who'd never seen
A coal-black giant in a velvet vest.
At first they'd shyly stared at you, afraid,
Till from your rum-barrel chest
Colossal chuckles came—
The people hurled their windows wide to watch
You stride, drum-major merry as your name.
To travel with you was to be your guest.

At school-year's end, an all-night boat from Wales
Had tossed us into Ireland, where we strode
Dear dirty Dublin in the shivering dawn,
And when we asked her in American
Where to find breakfast, a bewildered crone
Said, "Ah, you want the Gresham"—swells,
She'd thought us, rife with bucks.
A major domo in carnationed tux
Gave us a look that raked us up and down:
Unshaven bums in tousled GI duds.
Christ, would he throw us out?
But no. Concealed behind a screen
From proper diners' view,
We gorged on cream and strawberries, grilled trout.

Cronies in Paris, fellow GI Bill
Freeloaders, how we chipped away at French,
You battling hard to wrap it round your tongue:
"My fuckin' ol' declensions won't declench.
These buggy verbs
Get on my nerves." Poor as two weasels, young,
We hosteled in Vienna. At the Prater

You braved a ride to show me you were brave.
The infernal contraption flipped you upside down
And flung you in a near-neck-snapping loop—
I still can hear your eardrum-shattering bellow.

I'd ask you, with your spectacles' wise stare,
For worldly counsel. Long you'd mull, pronounce
With owlish professorial air:
"When lovers, they're too tired,
A bit of loving and
Their furnaces get fired."

In Scotland you went hungry, so I lent
You fifty, long by dribs and dabs repaid
In letters from Chicago. Your last payment
Which you encouraged me to spend on Coors
Came in your final letter.
Silence, for you had ceased to be my debtor,
Though I continue, Jerry Christmas, yours.

Poor People in Church

after Arthur Rimbaud, "Les Pauvres à l'église"

On side aisles heated by their fetid breath,
Parked in oak pews, these poor slobs hoist their eyes
To the shimmering gold chancel where the choir
With twenty mouths mouths pious harmonies;

Sniffing warm candle wax like the perfume
Of fresh-baked bread, these beaten mongrels cringe
Happily before their master, the good Lord
On whom their proud, pathetic prayers impinge.

These past few days, God's slow death made them writhe;
Now, their knees glad to wear smooth grooves in oak,
Wrapped in strange cat-fur coats, the women tend
Nondescript brats that cry as if they'd croak.

Their slimy nipples bared, these slurpers of soup
With prayerful eyes who hardly ever pray
Watch the procession of a badass group
Of teenage sluts in hats cocked any whichway.

Outside lurk cold and hunger, husbands drunk;
In here there's peace, an hour before unnamed
Evils again. Around them, shaggy crones
Whine, whisper, talk through their noses, mentally maimed

Bums that you'd whiff and sidestep in the street,
Bewildered epileptics between attacks
Burying their beaks in missals old as sin,
Blind dolts whom dogs lead into cul de sacs.

All babble endless begging litanies,
Bitching to Christ who dreams in his remote

Window, his face bright yellow from stained glass,
High above sorry rascal and fat old goat,

Far from the stench of flesh and moldy clothes,
From a dumbshow vile and glum whose time is past:
Prayers prettified with flowery turns of phrase
And musty mumbo-jumbo recited fast.

Now from the naves wherein the sun expires
Step classy dames, silk ruffles all aflutter,
Who flash—O Jesus!—green and bilious smiles.
Long sallow fingers kiss the holy water.

Sonnet Beginning with a Line and a Half
Abandoned by Dante Gabriel Rossetti

Would God I knew there were a God to thank
    When thanks rise in me, certain that my cries
Do not like blind men's arrows pierce the skies
    Only to fall short of my quarry's flank.
Why do I thirst, a desperate castaway
    Quaffing salt water, powerless to stop,
Sick lark locked in a cellar far from day,
    Lone climber of a peak that has no top?

To praise God is to bellow down a well
    From which rebounds one's own dull booming voice,
        Yet the least leaf points to some One to thank.
The whorl embodied in the slightest shell,
    The firefly's glimmer signify Rejoice!
        Though overhead, clouds cruise a sullen blank.

God's Obsequies

So I went to the funeral of God,
A ten-Cadillac affair,
And sat in a stun. It seemed everyone
Who had helped do Him in was there:

Karl Marx had a wide smirk on his face;
Friedrich Engels, a simpering smile,
And Friedrich Nietzsche, worm-holed and leechy,
Kept tittering all the while.

There was Sigmund Freud whose couch had destroyed
The soul, there was Edward Gibbon,
And that earth-shaking cuss Copernicus
Sent a wreath with a sun-gold ribbon.

There were Bertrand Russell and a noisy bustle
Of founders of home-made churches,
And Jean-Paul Sartre bawling "Down with Montmartre!"
There were prayer-cards a dime could purchase,

There were Adam and Eve and the Seven Deadly Sins,
Buxom Pride in her monokini,
(Said Sloth, "Wake me up when the party begins"),
And Lust playing with his weenie.

Declared Martin Luther, ablaze with rancor,
"Why mourn ye, O hypocrites?
May the guilty be gored with Michael's sword!
It's the work of the Jesuits!"

Mused the Pope on the folding chair next to me
As he mopped his expiring brow,
"Whatever will become of the See of Rome?
Ah, who'll hire an old man now?"

I had a quick word with Jesus
In Aramaic and Greek.
"Yes," he said, "it's sad. And so sudden—why, Dad
Looked uncommonly well last week.

"But we all must go sometime, I warrant,
No matter how brief our careers.
It's a comfort to me to reflect that He
Had been getting along in years."

Then we all filed past the coffin
To pay our respects to the corse
And the first in line gave a gasp—"He's gone!
He must have dropped out of the hearse!"

"Good God!" cried the undertaker,
His face like a bucket of ash,
"As sure as I'm born, I could have sworn—
If this gets in the papers I'm trash."

I stumbled and groped out to open air,
Stared up at a blossoming tree
And the blooming thing still believed in spring,
As smug as a tree could be.

Passed a haystack. A buck-naked farmer
Was treading his doxie. She screamed.
"Not so loud," I said, "don't you know God's dead?"
But they just laughed—"Who'd have dreamed?"

The sun kept pursuing overhead
Its habitual endeavor,
And the bountiful earth rolled on, rolled on,
As though it might last forever.

Storehouse

Whenever you're away
I squirrel up a heap
Of unimportant news
That, still unshelled, I keep

To tell when you return
And meanwhile, since I lack
A listener in you,
Keep adding to the stack.

In days now I'll receive
From living through our rift
Your rich gift: that you'd take
Cracked acorns for a gift.

At the Antiques Fair

What monster combine harvested this grain
The dead held dear? Through silent living rooms
It crept relentless, separating rings
From hands they'd clung to. Threadbare uniforms
Of armies long disbanded, dolls that stare
With blind abandoned eyes, pisspots, decanters
It swept away, the ratty and the rare,
The stag that once had hats hung on his antlers.

The relatives made money. Now we traipse
Through a fun-house of unused Lifebuoy soap
Eighty years old, framed photographs of apes,
Dowries of linens yellowed. Unfulfilled hope
Hangs like a raincloud. On the make for gain,
We scavenge through the leavings of the slain.

Secret River

When love's done, drooped and drowned
    And buried, sleep flows by.
Scaled, tailed, and finetooth-boned,
    Descending, you and I
Have left our eyes upstairs,
    For what's there to remark?
Why interrupt with ears
    The dumbshow of the dark?

With finning hands we stir
    A petrifying river
Whose overhead and floor
    Extend to touch each other.
Opposing spears of stone,
    Limewater-rinsed, time-wrought,
We lengthen till we join
    Our inmost tips in thought.

Command Decision

The General glances over
Dispatches. Meadow clover
Transmuted to gold brick
On his croissant sits thick.
Decaffeinated fumes
Coruscate. He resumes
Stroking his kitten's cunt.
What tidings from the front?

Rumors are running rife:
Appreciable loss of life.
Though war's still undeclared
The capital has been spared.
Imperfect circumcisions
Have crippled four divisions
And several guided missiles
Have lost their warning whistles.

He sighs. Having read enough,
Regales himself with snuff.
A sensible man refuses
To care who wins, who loses
Or weep when victims suffer.
Wine is the one true buffer.
He pours. In the graveled yard
The rotting moon stands guard.

Bald Eagle

When the eagle has soared over eighty years old
And to zip up his fly has to perch on a chair,
When dragging one wing he descends the back stair
To empty his pot like a man panning gold,

He circles—bed to table, table to bed.
Can this dull rented room be an eagle's fate?
Bawls out the paperboy for being late.
His one true pleasure: counting out the dead.

Favoring the foot with all five toes,
A burnt cigar stub rotting in his beak,
He flaps his way slowly downtown to seek
Shrill talk with some old chickenhawk he knows.

Small boys limp after him. Oh what the hell,
How can it faze an eagle to be mocked?
No point in pegging stones at them, half-cocked.
They'd broadcast his peepee smell.

He scowls up Main Street. Nowhere to sit down.
Ought to have band concerts every week.
Even the clouds can't find a place to leak.
Why did he ever nest in such a town?

Now what takes shape inside his eggshell dome?
A sense of winter, each one like the last?
He circles and recircles moments past
And settles in his hollowness, at home.

Food nowadays: not like food used to be.
Misplaced, his lower plate. Spits out the upper.
Nowadays even he and whiskey don't agree.
From habit, without zest, he makes a supper

Of soup and mashed potatoes in his blender.
The sun swoops low, an ember of a torch.
He grooms his feathers, rocking on his porch,
Ready to face the full moon's unfurled splendor.

Meeting a Friend Again After Thirty Years

Take off that mask. I know it's you.
Those wrinkles, sunken chin,
And goggled eyes can't quite disguise
Your wry familiar grin.

This is our mutual Halloween.
As though we mean to scare,
We face each other through a screen
Of fake teeth, whitened hair.

Finding a Tintype

Still green, these boughs from which began
    Garlands of flesh: my Gran, who spread
    Twelve babies in her double bed
As one might open a fan,

While constant in baptismal black,
    Of every blessing, pound by pound,
    In this bouncing Bible goatskin-bound,
My grandfather kept track.

They died in hopes of early rise.
    Tucked between Scripture's sheets they slept
    Where Jacob's pinned-down angel kept
Watch by their couch with steelcut eyes

Through ninety winters, buried deep
    Till now. Their glances, crisp as sage,
    Rise from their good book's crumbling page,
Pressed fern fronds someone wished to keep.

Out of Tune with the Stars

Our stars today foretell
    A baleful horoscope:
In separate glooms to dwell,
    Abandoning all hope,

But blood in us demurs.
    We opt for ecstasy,
Out of tune with the stars
    And well content to be.

Envoi

Go, slothful book. Just go.
Fifty years slopping around the house in your sock-feet
Sucking up to a looking-glass
Rehearsing your face. Why
Don't you get a job?

Sing for one who will care
When words with a rhythm align.
Sing, but not contrive
Clear sense to rob.

Sing in the loosening hands
Of lovers who read late
While embers anguish underneath a grate.
Sing as your weight, abandoned then,
Crash-lands.

1985, 2006

Notes

This book selects what seems my less contemptible verse from previous collections and adds a rasher of items not collected before. To keep it trim, the selection omits any verse for children, epigrams, and things that seem primarily comic, not quite fit to call poetry. This latter sort will be found in *Peeping Tom's Cabin* (BOA Editions, fall 2007).

Ant Trap. "How You Gonna Keep 'Em Down on the Farm After They've Seen Paree?" by Sam Lewis, Joe Young, and Walter Donaldson, was a popular song of 1919. The detail of the grisly souvenir was suggested by Winfield Townley Scott's poem "The U.S. Sailor with the Japanese Skull" (1945).

Celebrations After the Death of John Brennan. This longer poem pays tribute to the most remarkable young poet I have known. John Michael Brennan, born in Denver in 1950, had been my student at Tufts, in Medford, Mass.; more often, I was his. In 1971 as a waiter at the Bread Loaf Writers' Conference, Brennan publicly accused longtime conference director John Ciardi of arrogance and not listening to the young; afterward, Ciardi resigned. There are accounts of this confrontation in L. Rust Hills, *The Craft of Writing* (1979), and Edward M. Cifelli, *John Ciardi* (1997). The year before his death, Brennan had dropped out of school to travel alone through England and Ireland. In summer 1972 he self-published his only book, *Air is*, a collection of poems, drawings, and photographs, some of which he had taken on his journey. In my poem italics indicate quotations from that book. Brennan returned to Tufts in the fall and enrolled in the College Within, an experimental program I taught in, whose director was Seymour Simches. Back home in Denver in February 1973, Brennan took his own life. On April 25, 1973, Carolyn Forché and other friends took part in an evening devoted to his memory.

Goblet. This version of Hofmannsthal's "Die Beiden" (The Two of Them) was written in friendly competition with Robert Bly. He had challenged poets who write in meter and rhyme to set him poems he could not translate better into open forms. Our two attempts appeared side by side in *Counter/Measures* Three (1974).

To Dorothy on Her Exclusion from *The Guinness Book of World Records*. The records listed are, or were, in *The Guinness Book*, even the claim that Helen of Troy (according to Christopher Marlowe's *Tragical History of Dr. Faustus*) launched more ships with her face than did any other woman in history. Prout was a nineteenth-century physicist who claimed to have named the atomic particle *proton* after himself. Whether or not justly, Guinness has credited Prout with giving his name to the largest number of objects in the universe.

The Ballad of Fenimore Woolson and Henry James. That a subtle history has been crudely simplified is a fair complaint, all the fairer if this ballad is read as strict biography. Certain details are invented, such as Fenimore's forwardness at the Hyde Park riots, and others have been left out. The main events are drawn from Leon Edel's account in *Henry James*, volumes 2 and 3 (1962–63), and from Lyndall Gordon's *The Private Life of Henry James* (1998). Cheryl B. Torsney, in *Constance Fenimore Woolson: The Grief of Artistry* (1989), maintains that Woolson suffered from depression, not from unrequited love. Whatever the truth, it seems clear that James, in shocked reaction to her death, felt that he might have prevented it.

In Part 2 of the ballad, stanzas 4–6 echo Woolson's letter from Florence in 1880 giving her first impressions of James. In fact, six years were to elapse between that letter and James's first stay under her roof. In Part 3, stanza 5 is based on a journal entry Woolson made shortly before her death. Both documents are given by Clare Benedict in *Constance Fenimore Woolson* (1930). Part 4 is now added. I am indebted to R. S. Gwynn for pointing out that I should have mentioned James's disposal of Fenimore's clothes. Gordon attributes this story to Mrs. Mercede Huntington, an aged American resident in Florence, who recalled that when she was a girl James had told it to her. In Part 5, stanza 6 derives from James's letter of 1907 following his last visit to Woolson's grave.

Rites. The late Mesolithic burial detailed in this poem took place in about 4,000 B.C. Dating of the mother's bones indicates that she was twenty years old. The Vedbaek discoveries are treated in Liv Nilsson Stutz's *Embodied Rituals and Ritualized Burials* (2003); they suggest that Mesolithic people may have held religious beliefs, perhaps a belief in immortality. For information, I am grateful to Vincent Butler of the School of Archaeology, University College Dublin.

Envoi. Slightly refurbished, this is the same "Envoi" that ended *Cross Ties*, a book of selected poems of 1985.

Index of Titles and First Lines

Titles are indicated in *italics*.

Credits

Two of the newly collected poems are old: "Death of a Window Washer" originally appeared in *Ontario Review* thanks to Raymond Smith and Joyce Carol Oates; "Pacifier," in the chapbook *Winter Thunder* (1990), published by Robert L. Barth. Others first appeared in these periodicals thanks to these poetry editors:

The Atlantic (David Barber), "Small House Torn Down To Build a Larger"

Columbia (Eric McHenry), "Innocent Times"

Cumberland Poetry Review (Eva Touster and others), "Epiphany"

Fulcrum (Philip Nicolayev and Katya Kapovich), "At the Antiques Fair," "Panic in the Carwash," "Poor People in Church"

Hampden-Sydney Poetry Review (Tom O'Grady), "Fireflies"

Iambs & Trochees (William F. Carlson), "Sonnet Beginning with a Line and a Half Abandoned by Dante Gabriel Rossetti"

Literary Imagination (Sarah Spence), "Uncertain Burial"

Measure (Paul Bone and Robert Griffith), "Brotherhood" (originally "Finding the Mousetrap")

The New Criterion (David Yezzi), "Finding a Tintype," "Meeting a Friend Again After Thirty Years"

New York Sun (Adam Kirsch), "Storehouse"

North Dakota Review (Donald Junkins), "Jerry Christmas"

Poetry (Joseph Parisi), "At Paestum," "Geometry" (Christian Wiman), "God's Obsequies"

The Sewanee Review (George Core), "Henry James after the Death in Venice of Constance Fenimore Woolson," now section 4 of "The Ballad of Fenimore Woolson and Henry James"

Smartish Pace (Stephen Reichert), "Silent Cell Phones"

Southwest Review (Willard Spiegelman), "Furnished Rental"

Several of these items appeared in a chapbook, *The Seven Deadly Virtues* (published by David Leightty) (Scienter Press, 2005), which first included "Secret River."

Poetry Titles in the Series